"The prerogative of a man is to command . . . the prerogative of a woman is to obey." So said Mr. Bumble in Charles Dickens' *Oliver Twist*. It was a view shared by most men in the nineteenth century, and by most women as well. For hundreds of years women had been taught that they were physically and mentally inferior to men. The law reinforced this lesson: an unmarried woman was subject to her father until she became twenty-one; when she married, at whatever age, control passed to her husband, who at once became the owner of all her possessions.

Using an exciting range of contemporary documents, the author surveys the position of women from the earliest days of the Industrial Revolution. He shows how a "Women's Movement" got under way to raise the status of the "weaker sex"—a movement which Queen Victoria called "this mad wicked folly". A major outcome of its long, often bitter struggle to win equality, fought by the Pankhursts and others, was the enfranchisement of women in 1918–28.

The story of this "petticoat rebellion" is brought right up to date. A look at the social position of women today makes it clear that, although better off than ever before, they still have causes for complaint, for much remains to be achieved in the economic sphere where the cry now is for equal pay and job opportunities with men.

Illustrated throughout with contemporary pictures, this new WAYLAND DOCUMENTARY HISTORY title contains many key extracts from parliamentary debates, government reports, speeches, letters, diaries, novels, newspapers, pamphlets, poems and songs.

Frontispiece Militant Suffragettes advertising a "Votes for Women" meeting near the House of Commons

Women's Rights

Patrick Rooke

"The demand for the vote is the greatest step
towards freedom which the human race
has ever yet made."—*Millicent Fawcett.*

"I am opposed to women voting as men
vote. I call it immoral, because I think the
bringing of one's women, one's mothers and
sistes and wives, into the political arena
disturbs the relations between sexes."—
HilaireBelloc.

WAYLAND PUBLISHERS LONDON

SBN 85340 182 9
Copyright © 1972 by Wayland (Publishers) Ltd
101 Grays Inn Road London WC1

Filmset by Keyspools Ltd, Golborne, Lancs.
Printed by C. Tinling & Co. Ltd, Prescot and London

Contents

List of Illustrations

1 The Weaker Sex

WHEN, in Charles Dickens's *Oliver Twist* (1838), Mr. Bumble told his newly-acquired wife that "the prerogative of a man is to command . . . the prerogative of a woman to obey", he was expressing a view held by nearly all men and women in Britain during the nineteenth century. The Church was of the same opinion: in the marriage ceremony, while each partner had to promise to "love, comfort and honour" the other, the woman was further required to "obey and serve" her husband (*The Book of Common Prayer*).

To honour and obey

The law made it clear that women had a lower status. If unmarried, a woman was under the control of her father until she reached the age of twenty-one; when married, at whatever age, control passed to her husband who straightway became the owner of all her possessions, as well as having the right to beat her and use her as he wished. In George Eliot's novel *Middlemarch* (1872) we find Mr. Casaubon warning Dorothea, his wife, that she has been exceeding her duties:

"Dorothea, my love, this is not the first occasion, but it were well that it should be the last, on which you have assumed a judgment on subjects beyond your scope. Into the question how far conduct, especially in the matter of alliances, constitutes a forfeiture of family claims, I do not now enter. Suffice it, that you are not here qualified to discriminate. What I now wish you to understand is, that I accept no revision, still less dictation within that range of affairs which I have deliberated upon as distinctly and properly mine. It is not for you to interfere between me and Mr. Ladislow, and still less to encourage communications from

11

Opposite Charles Dickens reading to his daughters. Although in many ways a great social reformer, Dickens had little sympathy with the movement for women's rights

him to you which constitute a criticism on my procedure."

Women in the middle ages

For hundreds of years it had been accepted that women were physically and mentally inferior to men. As early as the twelfth century Gratian, a Benedictine monk, commented on this inferiority, saying that it arose from the fact that unlike Man, "Woman was not made in God's image." It followed, therefore, as "a natural human order that the women should serve their husbands and the children their parents; for there is no justice where the greater serves the less." *(Corpus Juris Canonici)*. He believed that when a wife failed her husband, the man had the right to correct her.

Thomas More, nearly four hundred years later, also agreed that husbands should "chastise their wives". Like Gratian, he compared the relationship between husband and wife to that between parent and child: "In the holy days that be the last days of the months and years, before they come to the church, the wives fall down before their husband's feet at home and the children before the feet of their parents, confessing and acknowledging themselves offenders either by some actual deed, or by omission of their duty, and desire pardon of their offence." *(Utopia, 1516)*.

Eve the temptress

Often it was argued that women were more wicked than men. Had not Eve tempted Adam, and brought upon the human race the curse of Original Sin? Men must be wary of this female sinfulness and do all in their power to keep it in check. The deceitfulness of women was shown in the Old Testament story of Samson and Delilah:

Delilah's deceit

"And it came to pass afterward, that he loved a woman in the valley of Sorek, whose name was Delilah.

"And the lords of the Philistines came up unto her, and said unto her, Entice him, and see wherein his great strength lieth, and by what means we may prevail against him, that we may bind him to afflict him: and we will give thee everyone of us eleven hundred pieces of silver.

"And Delilah said to Samson, Tell me, I pray thee, wherein thy great strength lieth . . .

"And it came to pass, when she pressed him daily with her words, and urged him, so that his soul was vexed unto death;

Thomas More, who in his *Utopia*, advocated the complete subjection of
women to their husbands

"That he told her all his heart, and said unto her, There hath not come a razor upon mine head; for I have been a Nazarite unto God from my mother's womb: if I be shaven, then my strength will go from me, and I shall become weak, and be like any other man.

"And when Delilah saw that he had told her all his heart, she sent and called for the lords of the Philistines, saying, Come up this once, for he hath shewed me all his heart. Then the lords of the Philistines came up unto her, and brought money in their hand.

"And she made him sleep upon her knees; and she called for a man, and she caused him to shave off the seven locks of his head; and she began to afflict him, and his strength went from him." (*Book of Judges,* Chapter 16).

Mischievous woman In the sixteenth century, Robert Richardson, writing from a convent in Paris, warned, Woman "has always been the most conspicuous mischief of the human race. For she is an animal prouder than the lion, that fiercest and proudest of the brute creation—more wanton than the ape, more venomous than the asp, more false and deceitful than the syren. Nor can any of the fiercest beasts be worthily compared with the feminine monster. The lions feared Daniel in their den, and so did the dragon; yet mad Jezebel slew the righteous Naboth. Jonas escaped safe from the whale's belly; yet Samson, stoutest of mankind, escaped not the hands of his own wife. John Baptist lived many years unhurt among dragons and asps; yet Herodias no sooner knew him than she slew him." (*Commentary on the Rule of St. Augustine,* 1530).

Even more ferocious was the attack levelled against women by the fifteenth century witchcraft inquisitor Jacob Sprenger. Most women, he ranted, were servants of the Devil, responsible for the overthrow of nearly all the kingdoms of the world:

"Woman is a wheedling and secret enemy. And that she is more perilous than a snare does not speak of the snare of hunters, but of devils. For men are caught not only through their carnal desires, when they see and hear women: For S. Bernard says: Their face is as a burning wind, and their voice the hissing of serpents: but they also cast wicked spells on countless men and animals. And when it is said that her heart is a net, it speaks of the inscrutable malice which reigns in their hearts. And her hands are as bands for binding, for when they place their hands on a creature to bewitch it, then with the help of the devil they perform their design." *(Hammer of Witches, c.*1485).

William Shakespeare portrays the treachery of women in several of his plays, such as *Macbeth, King Lear* and *Hamlet.* In *Hamlet* (1602) the hero complains about the moral weakness of his mother, who has remarried within a month of his father's death: "Frailty, thy name is woman! . . . A beast, that wants discourse of reason, would have mourn'd longer." *Shakespeare on women*

Alexander Pope, the English poet, writing in the eighteenth century, declared "Most women have no characters at all." *(Moral Essays,* 1731–4).

But not all men had as low an opinion of women. Many justified their superior position on the grounds that women were delicate, gentle creatures who, being naturally submissive, needed male protection. Something of this attitude can be seen in this passage by Giovanni Boccaccio: *Boccaccio*

"It is a hard and hateful thing to see proud men, not to speak of enduring them. But it is annoying and impossible to suffer proud women, because in general Nature has given men proud and high spirits, while it has made women humble in character and submissive, more apt for delicate things than for ruling. Therefore, it should not be surprising if God's wrath is swifter and the sentence more severe against proud women whenever it happens that they surpass the boundaries of their weakness." *(Concerning Famous Women)*.

Jean-Jacques Rousseau, the French philosopher, said in *Emile* (1762) that women should make an effort to cultivate a docile manner: "Forced to obey a creature as imperfect as man, a creature often vicious and always faulty, she should learn to submit to injustice and to suffer the wrongs inflicted on her by her husband without complaint; she must be gentle for her own sake, not his." *Rousseau*

Rousseau, though a revolutionary thinker on many social matters, did little to improve the status of women. Indeed, he thought that a young girl should be educated to accept her subordinate place in society. It was as if, like John Milton in

15

Samson Agonistes, he imagined that male superiority was decreed by the Creator:

Therefore God's universal Law
Gave to the man despotic power
Over his female in due awe.

The many new social ideas put forward by the French philosopher, Jean-Jacques Rousseau, did not include an improvement in the status of women

However, relationships between the sexes were not the result of some supernatural law. The inferior status of women had largely been brought about by the transformation of society in Norman times, when, under a feudal regime, land was awarded in return for military service. This change depressed the position of a woman, for, unable to give such service, she became more and more dependent upon a man for protection. By the nineteenth century, when society was again facing sweeping changes—now the outcome of industrialization—many of the older attitudes towards women still remained.

NB

Just what Victorians thought about women can be seen in the novels of Charles Dickens, where they tend to fall into three categories—fools, shrews and angels. Amongst the women in the first of these groups is Flora Finching, whom time had made both physically unattractive and stupid:

Charles Dickens

"Flora, always tall, had grown to be very broad too, and short of breath; but that was not much. Flora, whom he had left a lily, had become a peony; but that was not much. Flora, who had seemed enchanting in all she said and thought, was diffuse and silly. That was much. Flora, who had been spoiled and artless long ago, was determined to be spoiled and artless now. That was a fatal blow." *(Little Dorrit,* 1857).

The following joke from *Punch* (1871), typical of many, was based on the belief that women frequently behaved in a foolish and illogical way:

Artless Woman: "Henry, dear, I want to go a little farther, to do some shopping. Let us take a cab."

Wretch: "Yes my love, and pick one with a nice respectable-looking driver, who we are quite sure hasn't just been carrying any patient to the Smallpox Hospital."

Artless Woman: "O, what a horrid idea! Ugh! It never occurred to me. Rather than run such a risk as that, I would walk."

The deluded Wife walks a mile and a half, and her deceitful Husband saves eighteenpence."

In spite of the prevailing view that a wife should obey her husband, there were some women who refused to bow to male domination. Dickens pictured several in his novels, one such

"EMPLOYMEN

A nineteenth-century cartoon showing the general (male) concept of women as pretty but empty-headed simpletons

OF WOMEN?

virago appearing in *Great Expectations* (1862):

"My sister, Mrs. Joe Gargery, was more than twenty years older than I, and had established a great reputation with herself and the neighbours because she had brought me up "by hand". Having at that time to find out for myself what the expression meant, and knowing her to have a hard and heavy hand, and to be much in the habit of laying it upon her husband as well as upon me, I supposed that Joe Gargery and I were both brought up by hand . . .

"My sister, Mrs. Joe, with black hair and eyes, had such a prevailing redness of skin, that I sometimes used to wonder whether it was possible she washed herself with a nutmeg-grater instead of soap. She was tall and bony, and almost always wore a coarse apron . . .

"'Mrs. Joe has been out a dozen times, looking for you, Pip. And she's out now, making it a baker's dozen.'

"'Is she?'

"'Yes, Pip,' said Joe; 'and what's worse, she's got Tickler with her.'

"At this dismal intelligence, I twisted the only button on my waistcoat round and round, and looked in great depression at the fire. Tickler was a wax-ended piece of cane, worn smooth by collision with my tickled frame."

Many of Dickens's women were neither fools nor shrews, but were gentle creatures with angelic natures. Of Rose Maylie in *Oliver Twist* (1838) he wrote:

"The younger lady was in the lovely bloom and springtime of womanhood; at that age, when, if ever angels be for God's good purposes enthroned in mortal forms, they may be, without impiety, supposed to abide in such as hers.

"She was not past seventeen. Cast in so slight and exquisite a mould; so mild and gentle; so pure and beautiful; that earth seemed not her element, nor its rough creatures her fit companions."

Male chauvinism

But though, like Dickens, Victorians often idealised women in this way, most men firmly refused to think of them as equals. Before the struggle for women's rights could gather momentum, it had to force a path through male hostility and prejudice.

20

2 The Movement Begins

THE FEMINIST MOVEMENT in Britain is usually thought to have *Mary* started in 1792 with the appearance of Mary Wollstonecraft's *Wollstonecraft* *A Vindication of the Rights of Woman.* Although there were earlier demands by women for an improvement in their status, these made little impact. Amongst such pleas was a pamphlet called *Woman not Inferior to Man* (1739), the identity of its author being hidden behind the pen-name of "Sophia, a Person of Quality". The pamphlet was a justification of "the natural Rights of the Fair Sex to a perfect Equality of Power, Dignity, and Esteem, with the Men."

Sophia declared: "Was every individual Man to divulge his thoughts of our sex, they would all be found unanimous in thinking, that we are made for their use, that we are fit only to breed and nurse children in their tender years, to mind household affairs, and to obey, serve and please our masters, themselves."

Mary Wollstonecraft (1759–97) was the second in a family of six children. Her father was wealthy by standards of the day, having inherited £10,000 from his father. But he was a spendthrift and drunkard. He terrorised the Wollstonecraft household and often beat his wife. Little wonder that the young Mary was unimpressed with talk about the sanctity of marriage.

After her mother died in 1780 she left home to become variously employed as needlewoman, paid companion, school teacher, governess, translator and author. Her life as an adult appears to have been no happier than her childhood and twice she attempted suicide.

Though she wrote several books, it is for her *Vindication,* completed in six weeks, that she will be remembered. The book found little favour at the time, however, and led Horace Walpole to call her a "hyaena in petticoats". In it she protested: "Women are told from their infancy, and taught by the example of their mothers, that a little knowledge of human weakness, justly termed cunning, softness of temper, *outward* obedience, and a scrupulous attention to a puerile kind of propriety, will obtain for them the protection of man; and should they be beautiful, everything else is needless."

When the poet John Milton tells us, she went on, "that women are formed for softness and sweet attractive grace, I cannot comprehend his meaning, unless he meant to deprive us of souls, and insinuate that we were beings only designed by sweet attractive grace, and docile blind obedience, to gratify the senses of man when he can no longer soar on the wing of contemplation.

"How grossly do they insult us who thus advise us only to render ourselves gentle, domestic brutes!"

Mary also attacked Rousseau for declaring "that a woman should never for a moment feel herself independent, that she should be governed by fear to exercise her *natural* cunning, and made a coquettish slave in order to render her a more alluring object of desire, a *sweeter* companion to man, whenever he chooses to relax himself."

If we look at history, she wrote, "we shall find that the women who have distinguished themselves have neither been the most beautiful nor the most gentle of their sex."

Female weakness
Mary Wollstonecraft blamed the weakness of women on their ignorance, and pleaded for more educational opportunities for her sex. The woman who "exercises her mind will, by managing her family and practising various virtues, become the friend, and not the humble dependent of her husband." (*Vindication*, 1792).

We cannot be sure why women began their movement for equality at this particular time. Without doubt, the growth of industrialization played an important part, for it radically altered the way of life for many women in both the middle and working classes. An increasing number of middle class women enjoyed a new prosperity, which enabled them to make more use of domestic servants and purchase from a wider range of manufactured goods. They found that they had spare time on their hands. The more dynamic began to turn their attention to matters outside their homes. It was this class that became the backbone of feminism. The frustration often felt by such women is conveyed by Charlotte Brontë in *Jane Eyre* (1847):

Jane Eyre

"It is vain to say human beings ought to be satisfied with tranquillity: they must have action; and they will make it if they cannot find it. Millions are condemned to a stiller doom than mine, and millions are in silent revolt against their lot. Nobody knows how many rebellions besides political rebellions ferment in the masses of life which people earth. Women are supposed to be very calm generally: but women feel just as men feel; they need exercise for their faculties, and a field for their efforts as much as their brothers do; they suffer from too rigid a constraint, too absolute a stagnation, precisely as men suffer; and it is narrow-minded in their more privileged fellow-creatures to say that they ought to confine themselves to making puddings and knitting stockings, to playing the piano and embroidering bags. It is thoughtless to condemn them, or laugh at them, if they seek to do more or learn more than custom has pronounced necessary for their sex."

For women in the working classes the Industrial Revolution had rather different effects. By helping to break up domestic crafts, it forced many of these women, for the first time, to look for work away from the home, in factory or mine. One writer, in 1833, gave this graphic description of life in the new factories:

Industrial Revolution

"The mode of life which the system of labour . . . forces upon the operative, is one singularly unfavourable to domesticity. Rising at or before day-break, between four and five o'clock the year round, scarcely refreshed by his night's repose, he swallows a hasty meal, or hurries to the mill without taking any food whatever. At eight o'clock, half an hour, and in some instances forty minutes, are allowed for breakfast. In many cases, the engine continues at work during mealtime, obliging the labourer to eat and still overlook his work . . . After this he is increasingly engaged—not a single minute of rest or relaxation being allowed him.

"At twelve o'clock the engine stops, and an hour is given for

A rather romanticized picture of matchgirls at work in a factory in the East End of London, 1871

dinner. The hands leave the mill, and seek their homes, where this meal is usually taken . . . If, as it often happens, the majority of the labourers reside at some distance, a great portion of the allotted time is necessarily taken up by the walk, or rather run, backwards and forwards . . .

"Again they are closely immured from one o'clock till eight or nine, with the exception of twenty minutes, this being allotted for tea, or baggin-time, as it is called. This imperfect meal is almost universally taken in the mill: it consists of tea and wheaten bread, with very few exceptions. During the whole of this long period they are actively and unremittingly engaged in a crowded room and an elevated temperature, so that, when finally dismissed for the day, they are exhausted equally in body and mind.

"It must be remembered that father, mother, son, and daughter, are alike engaged; no one capable of working is spared to make home (to which, after a day of such toil and privation, they are hastening) comfortable and desirable." (Peter Gaskell, *Manufacturing Population of England,* 1833).

The second half of the eighteenth century witnessed two events, the American and French Revolutions, which were symptomatic of a mounting demand for personal freedom to be found in several countries. This spirit was captured in Tom Paine's *The Rights of Man* (1791), from which Mary Wollstonecraft had derived the title of her book. Paine wrote: "Every history of the Creation, and every traditionary account, whether from the lettered or unlettered world, however they may vary in their opinion or belief of certain particulars, all agree in establishing one point, *the unity of* man; by which I mean that men are all of *one degree,* and consequently that all men are born equal, and with equal natural rights."

Women, like their menfolk, were stirred by such sentiments.

As well as this spirit of freedom, there were at this time signs of a growing desire amongst people to help those less fortunate than themselves. These humanitarians included women. Although many women taking part in these activities showed little interest in the feminist cause, and often fiercely opposed it, they did help the movement's progress, partly by directly helping to improve the lives of many women and girls, and partly by showing that women could be other than mere gentle, domestic creatures. *Humanitarian movement*

One such person was Hannah More (1745–1833), who provided schools for the children of the poor. She refused to read Mary Wollstonecraft's book, though this did not stop her from attacking it. Indeed, several years before its publication, Hannah More had already condemned those who wanted rights for women: *Hannah More*

"The imposing term of *rights* has been produced to sanctify the claims of our female pretenders, with a view not only to rekindle in the minds of women a presumptious vanity dishonourable to their sex, but produced with a view to excite in their hearts an

Hannah More worked hard to provide schools for poor children and other
social reforms, but she had little time for femininists

Elizabeth Fry visiting Newgate, in 1818. It was through her efforts that
the barbarous conditions in English jails were gradually improved

impious discontent with the post which God assigned them in
this world . . . A little Christian humility and sober-mindedness
are worth all the wild metaphysical discussion which has un-
settled the peace of vain women, and forfeited the respect of
reasonable men." *(Strictures on Female Education,* 1779).

Another outstanding woman was Elizabeth Fry (1780–1845), *Elizabeth Fry*
the famous Quaker, who worked hard to better the conditions
for female prisoners at Newgate Prison. She described her first
visit to Newgate in 1813: "All I tell thee is a faint picture of the
reality; the filth, the closeness of the rooms, the ferocious

27

manners and expressions of the women towards each other, and the abundant wickedness which everything bespoke, are quite indescribable." (Quoted by J. Adshead, *Prisons and Prisoners*, 1845).

Towards the end of her life she antagonised Elizabeth Stanton, who was to become one of America's leading feminists, by her pointed criticism of Lucretia Mott, already well-known as an American fighter for women's rights. Many years later Elizabeth Stanton wrote:

"If Mrs. Mott was conversing with a circle of friends on the lawn, Mrs. Fry would glide into the house. If Mrs. Mott entered at one door, Mrs. Fry walked out the other . . . Elizabeth Fry was not afraid to mingle in Newgate Prison with the scum of the earth,

Through the efforts of Mary Carpenter the first reform schools for young offenders were started in the 1850s. For the first time, children convicted of crime did not have to go to prison

but she was afraid to touch the hem of Lucretia Mott's garment."
(*History of Women's Suffrage*, 1881).

Mary Carpenter (1807–77) was a campaigner on behalf of *Mary Carpenter* juvenile delinquents and "children of the perishing and dangerous classes". She opposed sending young offenders to prison, where they mixed with hardened criminals. Instead, she wanted to see the establishment of reformatory schools. She told of a beautiful girl of 6 or 7 who appeared in a Liverpool court charged with begging, an activity forced upon her by her mother. Mary Carpenter reported the words of the magistrate that heard the case:

" 'What a dreadful calamity is that, that I have no place to send this child to. I believe I must commit her to gaol for 21 days, as the safest place for the child, and removing her from the protection of her mother.' And the child was accordingly sent to gaol." (*Reformatory Schools for Children*, 1851).

She wrote that, as a rule, "Girls placed under favourable circumstances are less prone to evil than boys, yet that in the degraded classes we are considering, they sink even lower than children of the other sex, and that their very natures appear more completely perverted; that the present system adopted towards Juvenile Delinquents is even more certain to prove their ruin than that of boys . . .

"The girl is kept at home to be the drudge, not the helpmate of the mother . . . she cannot in general be spared to go to school . . .

"The boys in the same families have been equally neglected, but the greater vigour of their natures has carried them into the open air . . . though equally unprincipled with the girls, and more prone to overt and daring mischief and crime, they have far more which can be worked on for good." (*Juvenile Delinquents*, 1853).

The most famous woman social reformer of the nineteenth *Florence* century was Florence Nightingale (1820–1910), who greatly *Nightingale* improved the status of nursing and helped to make it a respectable profession for women. Although she held her sex in low regard, as can be seen in the extract below, she did support many aspects of the women's movement. In a letter to Mary Clarke, a friend who had just written a book in which the nature of women had been discussed, Florence Nightingale wrote:

29

Florence Nightingale. A sketch made in Scutari, June 1856. Jerry Barrett.

"You say 'Women are more sympathetic than men.' Now if I were to write a book out of my experience, I should begin, *Women have no sympathy.* Yours is the tradition—mine is the conviction of experience. I have never found one woman who has altered her life by one iota for me or my opinions . . .

"My doctrines have taken no hold among women. Not one of my Crimean following learnt anything from me—or gave herself for one moment, after she came home, to carry out the lesson of that war, or of those hospitals. I have lived with a sister 30 years, with an aunt four or five, with a cousin two or three. Not one has altered one hour of her existence for me. Not one has read one of my books so as to be able to save me the trouble of writing or telling it all over again . . .

"It makes me mad the 'Woman's Rights' talk about the 'want of a field' for them—when I know that I would gladly give £500 a year for a Woman Secretary . . . And we can't get one . . .

"Women crave for *being loved,* not for loving. They scream at you for sympathy all day long, they are incapable of giving any in return, for they cannot remember your affairs long enough to do so . . .

"I am sick with indignation at what wives and mothers will do of the most egregious selfishness. And people call it all maternal or conjugal affection, and think it pretty to say so. No, no, let each person tell the truth from his own experience."

Caroline Norton (1808–77) was a very different sort of person, *Caroline Norton* though like Hannah More she was no feminist. In a letter to the *Examiner* in 1838 she declared: "I believe in the natural superiority of man, as I do in the existence of God . . . I never pretended to the wild and ridiculous doctrine of equality."

Caroline was extremely beautiful, with dark eyes and hair, and loved the life of fashionable society. When nineteen, she married George Norton, a younger brother of Lord Grantley, but relations between the couple soon soured, even to the point of them quarrelling in public. At last, in 1836, George Norton decided on divorce. He refused to let Caroline inside his house and would not allow her to see their three sons—something he was legally entitled to do. Then, in pursuit of the divorce, he brought an action for alienation of his wife's affections against

31

Opposite Florence Nightingale showed that women were fully capable of hard, responsible work

Lord Melbourne, the Prime Minister, who was a close friend of Caroline. The nation was shocked and for a time it seemed that Melbourne would have to resign. However, the suit failed and the Prime Minister's name was cleared. But though it also proved Caroline's innocence, it did nothing to reunite her with her sons.

Frustrated and angry, she now began to campaign for a mother's right to have custody of her children, a fight in which she was supported by Thomas Talfourd, M.P. for Reading. Talfourd introduced an Infants' Custody Bill into Parliament which finally became law in 1839. The Act allowed a mother, against whom adultery had not been proved, to keep the custody of all children under the age of seven, and to have regular access to any who were older.

Marriage and divorce: Gladstone

Later, Caroline worked to bring about a reform of the Marriage and Divorce Laws, her efforts contributing to the passage of a new Act in 1857. The Liberal, William Gladstone, was amongst the fiercest opponents of this measure:

"As soon as the Bill came down to the House of Commons Mr. Gladstone hastened up to London . . . [where] he found the counsels of his friends by no means encouraging for the great fight on which he was intent. They deprecated anything that would bring him into direct collision with Lord Palmerston. They urged that violent opposition now would be contrasted with his past silence, and with his own cabinet responsibility for the very same proposal. Nothing would be intelligible to the public, Lord Aberdeen said, beyond a 'carefully moderated course'. But a carefully moderated course was the very last thing possible to Mr. Gladstone when the flame was once kindled, and he fought the Bill with a holy wrath as vehement as the more worldly fury with which Henry Fox, from very different motives, had fought the marriage Bill of 1753 . . .

"The discussion of the Bill in the Commons occupied no fewer than eighteen sittings, more than one of them, according to the standard of those primitive times, inordinately long . . . On every division those who affirmed the principle of the Bill were at least two to one. 'All we can do,' Gladstone wrote to his wife, 'is to put shoulder to shoulder, and this, please God, we will do . . . Yesterday, ten-and-a-half hours, rather angry; today with pacification,

William Gladstone was one of the fiercest opponents of rights for women.
Ironically, he sat as a Liberal member of Parliament

but still tough and prolonged'. An unfriendly but not wholly unveracious chronicler says of this ten hours' sitting (August 14th) on a single clause: 'Including questions, explanations, and interlocutory suggestions, Mr. Gladstone made nine-and-twenty speeches, some of them of considerable length. Sometimes he was argumentative, frequently ingenious and critical, often personal, and not less often indignant at the alleged personality of others'." (John Morley, *Life of Gladstone,* 1903).

The Marriage and Divorce Act of 1857 protected, for the first time, the earnings of a wife deserted by her husband; it gave a wife the right to inherit or bequeath wealth just as a single woman could; and it enabled a wife who was separated from her husband to take various kinds of legal action on her own behalf.

Caroline Norton was no feminist, and her activities on behalf of married women stemmed in the main from a sense of personal injury. Yet she succeeded in helping her sex to win a legal recognition which they had not had before.

3 *The Right to Vote*

R. J. RICHARDSON, in a pamphlet written at Lancaster Prison in 1840, declared: "Bad laws will never cease to be, nor wicked legislation cease to rule, until every man of twenty-one years of age, and every woman of twenty, obtain, by their strenuous exertions, a voice in the election of those whom reason and honesty qualify for law-makers and administrators." [1]

The battle for political rights was to become an important part of the women's movement. Throughout the nineteenth century, against the background of a noisy campaign for universal manhood suffrage, a growing body of women also demanded the right to vote in parliamentary and municipal elections. The laws of Britain are made by men, these female rebels argued; not until we have a voice in the law-making processes will our subservient state be ended.

Working-class women

Early in the century many working-class women fought alongside their menfolk for safer working conditions, shorter hours, against the Combination Laws, as well as for a reform of the franchise. A radical, Samuel Bamford, reported in 1818:

"With the restoration of the Habeas Corpus Act, the agitation for reform was renewed. Numerous meetings followed in various parts of the country . . . At one of these meetings, which took place at Lydgate, in Saddleworth, I, in the course of an address, insisted on the right, and the propriety also, of females who were present at such assemblages, voting by show of hand, for, or against the resolutions. This was a new idea; and the women, who attended numerously on that bleak ridge, were mightily pleased with it—and the men being nothing dissentient—when the

35

Women and children were among the victims of the Peterloo Massacre, 1819

37

resolution was put, the women held up their hands, amid much laughter; and ever from that time, females voted with the men at the radical meetings. I was not then aware, that the new impulse thus given to political movement, would in short time be applied to charitable and religious purposes. But it was so; our females voted at every subsequent meeting; it became the practice— female political unions were formed, with their chair-women, committees, and other officials." *(Passages in the Life of a Radical,* 1844).

Peterloo Massacre   Thousands of women were present at the infamous Peterloo Massacre in 1819. Bamford described the scene as the yeomanry charged: "On the breaking of the crowd, the yeomanry wheeled; and dashing wherever there was an opening, they followed, pressing and wounding. Many females appeared as the crowd opened; and striplings or mere youths also were found. Their cries were piteous and heart-rending; and would, one might have supposed, have disarmed any human resentment: but here, their appeals were vain. Women, white-vested maids, and tender youths, were indiscriminately sabred or trampled."

Violent women   Women demonstrators often showed that they could be as hostile towards authority as their husbands or brothers. Edward Hamer tells what happened when a crowd of Chartists, assembled at Llanidloes in 1839, became angry: three of its number had been arrested and taken to a nearby hotel by London police brought specially into the town:

"Some of the women who had joined the crowd kept instigating the men to attack the hotel—one old virago vowing that she would fight till she was knee-deep in blood, sooner than the Cockneys should take their prisoners out of the town. She, with others of her sex, gathered large heaps of stones, which they subsequently used in defacing and injuring the building which contained the prisoners." *(The Chartist Outbreak in Llanidloes,* 1867).

Women and Chartism   The Chartists demanded universal suffrage. For some, in the early days of Chartism, this meant votes for both men and women. Before long, however, it had a more limited meaning:

Mr. Doubtful: "I should be obliged by your informing me what is the meaning of the term Chartist."

Crowds watch the procession of Chartists taking their National Petition to the House of Commons. Universal suffrage was one of the Chartists' demands

Radical: "It is one who is an advocate for the People's Charter."

Mr. D: "The People's Charter, pray what is that?"

Radical: "It is the outline of an act of parliament, drawn up by a committee of the London Working Men's Association, and six members of parliament; and embraces the six cardinal points of Radical Reform."

Mr. D: "What are these points?"

Radical: "They are as follows: 1. *Universal suffrage*—2. *Annual Parliaments*—3. *Vote by Ballot*—4. *Equal Representation*—5. *Payment of Members*—6. *No Property Qualification.*"

Mr. D: "Do you mean by *Universal Suffrage,* that men, women, and children should vote?"

Radical: "No, we do not: it is often difficult to find a term which shall clearly express what you mean, and perhaps universal adult male suffrage would have been a more near approach to our meaning." *(Tract issued by the Finsbury Tract Society,* 1839).

Many working-class women supported the Chartist cause. They believed that if their men won the right to vote, this would lead to an improvement in their own lives. The following is part of an Address of the Female Political Union of Newcastle upon Tyne:

"Fellow-countrywomen, We call upon you to join us and help our fathers, husbands, and brothers, to free themselves and us from political, physical, and mental bondage, and urge the following reasons as an answer to our enemies and an inducement to our friends.

"We have been told that the province of woman is her home, and that the field of politics should be left to men; this we deny; the nature of things renders it impossible, and the conduct of those who give the advice is at variance with the principles they assert. Is it not true that the interests of our fathers, husbands and brothers, ought to be ours? If they are oppressed and impoverished, do we not share those evils with them? If so, ought we not to resent the infliction of those wrongs upon them? We have read the records of the past, and our hearts have responded to the historian's praise of those women, who struggled against tyranny and urged their countrymen to be free or die . . .

"We have seen that because the husband's earnings could not support his family, the wife has been compelled to leave her home neglected and, with her infant children, work at a soul and body degrading toil. We have seen the father dragged from his home by a ruffian press-gang, compelled to fight against those that never injured him, paid only 34 shillings per month, while he ought to have had £6; his wife and children left to starve or

"Home" to many thousands of poor workers and their families was one
room in a tenement. Water and sanitation were in the yard outside

subsist on the scanty fare doled out by hired charity. We have seen the poor robbed of their inheritance and a law enacted to treat poverty as a crime, to deny misery consolation, to take from the unfortunate their freedom, to drive the poor from their homes and their fatherland, to separate those whom God has joined together, and tear the children from their parents care— this law was passed by men and supported by men, who avow the doctrine that the poor have no right to live, and that an all wise and beneficient Creator has left the wants of his children unprovided for.

"For years we have struggled to maintain our homes in comfort, such as our hearts told us should greet our husbands after their fatiguing labours. Year after year has passed away, and even now our wishes have no prospect of being realised, our husbands are over wrought, our houses half furnished, our families ill-fed, and our children uneducated—the fear of want hangs over our heads; the scorn of the rich is pointed towards us; the brand of slavery is on our kindred, and we feel the degradation. We are a despised caste. Our oppressors are not content with despising our feelings, but demand the control of our thoughts and wants! . . .

"We have searched and found that the cause of these evils is the Government of the country being in the hands of a few of the upper and middle classes, while the working men who form the millions, the strength and wealth of the country, are left without the pale of the Constitution, their wishes never consulted, and their interests sacrificed by the ruling factions, who have created useless officers and enormous salaries for their own aggrandisement . . .

"We harbour no evil wishes against any one, and ask for nought but justice; therefore, we call on all persons to assist us in this good work, but especially those shopkeepers which the Reform Bill enfranchised. We call on them to remember it was the unrepresented working men that procured them their rights, and that they ought now to fulfil the pledge they gave to assist them to get theirs." *(Northern Star,* 2nd February, 1839).

Anne Knight

Amongst the middle class, at this time, no woman was more active in the campaign for political rights than Anne Knight, a

Quaker. She was delighted to discover in January, 1851—almost three years after the last, and disastrous, Chartist petition had been presented to Parliament—that a National Charter Association with women members was still in existence. She wrote to a Mrs. Rooke at the organization's headquarters in Sheffield:

"I take early opportunity of writing to beg those patriotic women as members of the National Charter Association to aid their brethren in the revising of the Charter, the first article of which is in error, calling that universal which is only half of it. It will now dishonour them to go on repeating their demand for only men when it is so widely spread and acknowledged that every adult member of the human family bearing the same burdens has the same right to a vote, for the man who makes the laws and taxes, which sisters as well as brothers are alike compelled to endure and pay."

Some men did speak out in favour of the women's cause. R. J. Richardson, a leading radical from Salford, wrote a pamphlet in support of *The Rights of Woman* (1840) whilst held a prisoner for his Chartist activities:

"Rights of Woman"

" 'Ought Women to interfere in the political affairs of the country?' . . . I do most distinctly and unequivocally say—YES! And for the following reasons:

"*First,* Because she has a natural right.

"*Second,* Because she has a civil right.

"*Third,* Because she has a political right.

"*Fourth,* Because it is a duty imperative upon her.

"*Fifth,* Because it is derogatory to the divine will to neglect so imperative a duty . . .

"It is nowhere written in the body of the civil law, that woman, by reason of her sex, is disqualified from the exercise of political right except by her own voluntary act. Grotius, Puffendorf, Montesquieu, Vattel, and other famous civilians, have nowhere consented to such an unjust exclusion; the only instance on record where we find this right disputed, is in the famous controversy between Philip of Valois, and Edward III, concerning the Salic law, by which females and their descendants are excluded from the monarchy of France, and from the inheritance of the allodial lands of the nobility; the latter part of the law has long

John Stuart Mill and his wife, Harriet, were two sincere and dedicated campaigners for women's rights

become obsolete, and the former is nowhere acted upon except in France, proving that the doctrine of the exclusion of females from political power is not consonant with the law of nature and nations...

"If a woman is qualified to be a Queen over a great nation, *Queen Victoria* armed with power of nullifying the powers of Parliament or the deliberate resolutions of the two estates of the realm, by parity of reason, a woman in a minor degree ought to have a voice in the election of the legislative authorities. If it be admissible that the Queen, a woman, by the constitution of the country can command, can rule over a nation (and I admit the justice of it) then I say, woman in every instance ought not to be excluded from her share in the Executive and legislative power of the country."

Richardson claimed that it was "a most incontrovertible fact, that women contribute to the wealth and resources of the kingdom," and went on to show in great detail the various kinds of work that they undertook. He concluded:

"I have now shown you that woman bears her share in the burdens of the state, and contributes more than her fair proportion to the wealth of the country. I ask you, is there a man, knowing these things, who can lay his hand upon his heart, and say, Woman ought not to interfere in political affairs? No: I hope there is none for the honour of my sex—I do sincerely hope there is none."

John Stuart Mill (1806–73) was a more famous male champion *John Stuart Mill* of women's rights. His wife, Harriet, was a leading feminist, and in 1851 wrote an article on *The Enfranchisement of Women* which appeared in the *Westminster Gazette*. Without doubt she influenced Mill's thinking on the grievances of her sex. His thoughts on women's suffrage were first set down in 1861:

"In the preceding argument for universal, but graduated suffrage, I have taken no account of difference of sex. I consider it to be entirely irrelevant to political rights as differences in height or in the colour of the hair. All human beings have the same interest in good government; the welfare of all alike is affected by it, and they have equal need of a voice in it to secure their share of its benefits. If there be any difference, women require it more than men, since, being physically weaker, they are more dependent on law and society for protection. Mankind has long since abandoned the only premises which will support the conclusion that women ought not to have votes.

"No one now holds that women should be in personal servitude; that they should have no thought, wish, or occupation, but to be the domestic drudges of husbands, fathers, or brothers. It is allowed to unmarried women, and wants but little of being conceded to married women, to hold property, and have pecuniary and business interests, in the same manner as men. It is considered suitable and proper that women should think, and write, and be teachers. As soon as these things are admitted, the political disqualification has no principle to rest on." (*Considerations on Representative Government*, 1861).

"Subjection of Women" In 1869, Mill wrote *The Subjection of Women* in which he asked why women had a lower social status than men: "All causes, social and natural, combine to make it unlikely that women should be collectively rebellious to the power of men. They are so far in a position different from all other subject classes, that their masters require something more from them than actual service. Men do not want solely the obedience of women—they want their sentiments. All men, except the most brutish, desire to have, in the woman most nearly connected with them, not a forced slave but a willing one, not a slave merely, but a favourite. They have therefore put everything in practice to enslave their minds. The masters of all other slaves rely, for maintaining obedience, on fear; either fear of themselves, or religious fears. The masters of women wanted more than simple obedience, and they turned the whole force of education to effect their purpose.

"All women are brought up from the very earliest years in the belief that their ideal of character is the very opposite to that of men; not self-will, and government by self-control, but submission, and yielding to the control of others. All the moralities tell them that it is the duty of women, and all the current sentimentalities that it is their nature, to live for others; to make complete abnegation of themselves, and to have no life but in their affections. And by their affections are meant the only ones they are allowed to have—those to the men with whom they are connected, or to the children who constitute an additional and indefeasible tie between them and man.

"When we put together three things—first, the natural attraction between opposite sexes; secondly, the wife's entire dependence on the husband, every privilege or pleasure she has being either his gift, or depending entirely on his will; and lastly, that the principal object of human pursuit, consideration, and all objects of social ambition, can in general be sought or obtained by her only through him—it would be a miracle if the object of being attractive to men had not become the polar star of feminine education and formation of character."

John Stuart Mill's election to Parliament as a Liberal, in 1865, caused a stir. He would not contribute any personal money to the election expenses, nor take part in any canvassing; he told the electors that he wanted women to have the franchise. It was something of a surprise, therefore, when he was returned to Westminster.

The magazine *Punch* was not unsympathetic to the women's claim for political rights. In the same year it published a poem attacking the radical John Bright. Why, it asked, was Bright merely campaigning for an extension of male suffrage:

Punch

WOMAN'S RIGHT: A BILLET TO BRIGHT

Dearest, could I use a warmer
Word, I would JOHN BRIGHT, *yet oh!*
But a half and half reformer,
Far enough thou dost not go.
Manhood's right to the elective
Suffrage thou proclaimest due;
Why, with logic so defective,
Womanhood's assert not too?

Voteless, working men contented
Should not rest, they're told by thee.
Tell us why, unrepresented,
Working women ought to be.
If deficient information
Is no hindrance in men's way

To a share in legislation,
We are quite as wise as they.

Saw, plane, chisel, are they better
Than the washtub and the churn?
If the pickaxe you unfetter,
Let the mangle have a turn.
Oh, JOHN, *you should get on faster!*
Woman's equal rights proclaim;
Treat the mistress like the master.
Won't you? Naughty man, for shame!

Reform Act
(1867)

During the lengthy and heated debates which led up to the Reform Act of 1867 some attempts were made to include the enfranchisement of women in the Bill. Mill moved an amendment to that effect, but with no success. Parliament received and rejected the first mass petition asking for women's suffrage. Women appeared to have gained an ally in the Conservative leader Benjamin Disraeli, when he told the House of Commons, "I do not see, when she has so much to do with the state and Church, on what reasons, if you come to right, she has not a right to vote." But, when Prime Minister, Disraeli did nothing to see that this right was granted.

The controversy over women's suffrage was commented upon by *Punch,* in 1867, by means of the following *conversazione:*

Professor Podgers: "Let me offer you a cigar."

Dr. Harriet Brown: "Thank you, no; I prefer a short pipe." *(Produces one, and lights it. They smoke.)*

Prof.: "What weather we have had!"

Dr. Harriet: "And what debates!"

Prof.: "When shall we have an atomospheric reform?"

Dr. H.: "Before we get Reform in Parliament."

Prof.: "When will that be?"

Dr. H.: "Not yet awhile. We shall get no Reform worthy of the name this Session."

48

Prof.: "Why?"

Dr. H.: "The House will reject Mr. Mill's Amendment."

Prof.: "And you will remain unenfranchised."

Dr. H.: "As long as we do there will be no real representation of the people, and to call the Reform Bill the Representation of the People Bill will be absurd. The people consists of women as well as men. Women are half of the people. If they are un-represented, the people can be but half represented."

Prof.: "Well, that no doubt is a bit of Mill's logic. But say that women are the better half of the people. They are already represented by their husband's votes."

Dr. H.: "Are they? Do you think, if they were, the property in-herited by wives would belong to their husbands?"

Prof.: "But are the majority of women fit to possess the suffrage?"

Dr. H.: "As fit as the majority of men. Reformers say that the Constitution wants repairing, and must be repaired by working-men. A good needlewoman is as able to mend the British Constitution as a journeyman carpenter."

Prof.: "Do you claim Womanhood Suffrage?"

Dr. H.: "Yes, if men are to have Manhood Suffrage. Isn't taxation without representation tyranny? We are taxed as well as men. We are subject to laws made without our consent. Show me any real reason why we should not vote."

Prof.: "I think I can mention one."

Dr. H.: "What is it?"

Prof.: "You ought not to exercise political rights because you are exempt from civic duties."

Dr. H.: "How so?"

Prof.: "You are not eligible to serve on juries."

Dr. H.: "I am willing to be."

Prof.: "Nor are you liable to be drawn for the Militia."

Dr. H.: "I am ready."

Prof.: "You cannot be Churchwardens, Overseers or Magis-trates."

Dr. H.: "I don't see why."

Prof.: "You cannot be Aldermen."

Dr. H.: "But we might be Alderwomen."

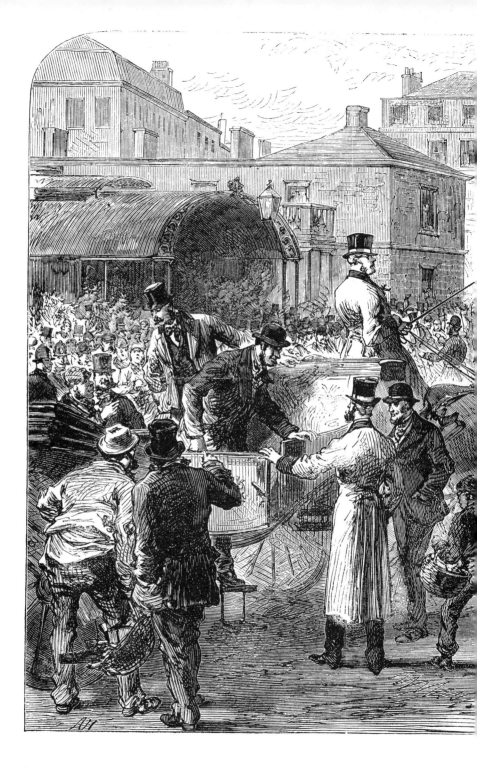

50

Men arriving to cast their votes in the general election of 1868. But suffrage was not yet universal; women could not vote

51

Prof.: "Some of you; and Mayoresses too. But not all. Not the generality. There are perhaps women fit to be Prime Ministers or Chancellors of the Exchequer. But are they not a small minority?"

Dr. H.: "There is certainly something in your objection to female suffrage."

Prof.: "Besides, if women are to vote, why should they be excluded from Parliament? Who but women could represent women?"

Dr. H.: "Well, I'll tell you what, then. Let there be a female Parliament. Constitute a Third House, and call it a House of Ladies. Make its assent necessary to all statutes affecting the interests of women."

Prof.: "That to be sure, would be a way out of the difficulty. Perhaps it will suggest itself to the Member for Westminster. Why is Mr. Mill like a tongue?"

Dr. H.: "Give it up."

Prof.: "Because he is the Ladies' Member."

4 Women at Work

THE CENSUS RETURNS for 1841 show that in England alone there were about two million working-women. By far the largest group of these, numbering nearly three-quarters of a million, were employed as domestic servants. Many others worked in the textile trades, over 100,000 working in the Lancashire cotton industry. Peter Gaskell compared the women in this last group with those who came from the more elevated sectors of Lancashire society:

"Lancashire has long been celebrated for the beauty of its women . . . In the higher and middle classes of society, there are certainly to be found many exquisite specimens of female loveliness—many exceedingly graceful and feminine beings. They may be seen in abundance in all the social circles, in places of amusement and parade, in which, like the sex all the world over, they naturally assemble—a passion for admiration and attention forming an essential and important part of woman's character, and one too of the utmost value, and worthy every cultivation.

"But these must not be sought for amongst the precociously developed girls herding in factories. Here, on the contrary, will be found an utter absence of grace and feminine manners—a peculiar raucous or rough timbre of voice—no such thing as speaking soft and low, 'that most excellent thing in woman', a peculiarity owing to various causes, a principal one of which is, too early sexual excitement, producing a state of vocal organs closely resembling that of the male.

"Here is no delicacy of figure, no 'grace in all her steps', no 'heaven within her eye', no elegance of tournure, no retiring

Factory women

53

Above Women at work in a power loom weaving shed, 1840. The view is idealized; few mills or factories were ever as clean and neat as this

Below A savage cartoon by Andrew Cruikshank on the lot of the women who had to work in the small, sweated labour industries

bashfulness, no coy reserve, no indication that a woman's soul dwells there in all its young loveliness, with its host of hidden delights, waiting but the touch of some congenial spirit to awaken all its sensibilities and passions; but in their place an awkward and ungainly figure;—limbs badly moulded from imperfect nutrition—a bony framework, in many points widely divergent from the line of womanly beauty—a beauty founded upon utility —a general aspect of coarseness and a vulgarity of expression quite opposed to all ideas of excellencies in the moral and physical attributes of her sex." (*The Manufacturing Population of England,* 1833).

Another writer referred to those who worked in the cotton mills as "this degraded class of our countrywomen." He wrote: "At an early age, even before their tender frames receive the nourishment and secretions necessary to befit them for the duties nature ordained they should perform in after life, many years before the age of puberty, are they taken to these hell-holes to earn their little pittance . . . Immured in these dens, oppressed by fatigue, fed with insufficient diet, their little minds abused, their bodies scourged, their frames wasted, the pith of womanhood dried up and withered, they grow up in years, in many instances deformed in body, or die prematurely with the first attack of disease. Some are women and mothers years before their natural period. But are they taken from these accursed mills by their husbands?—No! once a factory slave, seldom do they leave it but with death." (R. J. Richardson, *The Rights of Woman,* 1840).

Conditions in the mills were bad, but many women feared the loss of their jobs. In the discussion which preceded the Factory Act of 1833, it was proposed that women be excluded from the industry. When this was supported in the pages of *The Examiner* in 1832, it brought the following protest from the "Female Operatives of Todmorden":

Fear of unemployment

"Sir, Living as we do, in the densely populated manufacturing districts of Lancashire, and most of us belonging to that class of females who earn their bread either directly or indirectly by manufactories, we have looked with no little anxiety for your opinion on the Factory Bill . . . You are for doing away with our services in manufactories altogether. So much the better, if you had pointed out any other more eligible and practical employment for the surplus female labour, that will want other channels for subsistence. If our competition were withdrawn, and short hours substituted, we have no doubt but the effects would be as you have stated, "not to lower wages, as the male branch of the family would be enabled to earn as much as the whole had done," but for the thousands of females who are employed in manufactories, who have no legitimate claim on any male relative for employment or support, and who have, through a variety of circumstances, been early thrown on their own resources for a livelihood, what is to become of them? . . .

"It is a lamentable fact, that in these parts of the country, there is scarcely any other mode of employment for female industry, if we except servitude and dressmaking."

Some male observers thought that women were lucky to work in factories. To one writer these buildings were "spacious halls" where the beneficial "power of steam summons around him his myriads of willing menials and assigns to each the regulated task." (Andrew Ure, *The Philosophy of Manufactures,* 1835).

Another concluded that "One of the greatest advantages resulting from the progress of manufacturing industry, and from severe manual labour being superseded by machinery, is its tendency to raise the condition of women. Education only is wanting to place the women of Lancashire higher in the social scale than in any other part of the world." (W. Hickson, *Handloom Weavers' Report,* 1840).

Lace-runners For women employed in many of the smaller domestic industries life could be even more wretched than for those in the textile mills. Elizabeth Sweeting was a lace-runner; from her evidence to the Children's Employment Commission in 1843, we form this picture of her working conditions:

"Has worked at the trade twenty-one years. When she first began it was a very good business. Begins at 7 a.m., and leaves off about 10 p.m. but oftener later than earlier. Often works till between 11 and 12, has done so all the winter round. In the summer generally begins between 5 and 6, and works as long as it is light, often till 9 p.m. Often does not go to the bottom of the yard for a week. Can earn by working hard 7d *(3p.)* a day . . .

She has now a little girl helping, and together they can earn a shilling *(5p.)*. Finds her sight very much affected, so much that she cannot see what o'clock it is across her room. The work affects the stomach and causes a pain in the side; often makes her light-headed. Generally the lace-runners are crooked, so that the right shoulder is higher than the other."

The industrial system, it was claimed, produced women who were ignorant and neglectful of their families: "One of the greatest evils to the working man is the ignorance of the women of his own class, who are generally incapable of becoming either good wives or good mothers . . . Brought up in the factory until they are married, and sometimes working there long after that event has taken place, even when they have become mothers, they are almost entirely ignorant of household duties . . . [They] are incapable of laying out the money their husbands have earned to the best advantage. They are equally incapable of preparing his victuals, in an economical and comfortable manner; and not infrequently as much money is spent on a Sunday's dinner as in other and better hands would have procured a dinner for two or three days. A working man is fortunate, indeed, who happens to marry a young woman who has been brought up in service, and whose habits of cleanliness and knowledge of household duties secures him a comfortable home and economical management." (Factories Commission, *First Report,* 1833).

Of married women in the lace trade, a Report complained: "One of the most appalling features connected with the extreme reduction that has taken place in the wages of lace-runners, and the consequent long hours of labour, is that married women— having no time to attend to their families, or even to suckle their offspring freely administer opium in some form or other to their infants, in order to prevent their cries interfering with the protracted labour by which they strive to obtain a miserable subsistence." (Children's Employment Commission, 1843).

Nowhere were working conditions worse for women and girls than in Britain's coal mines. Betty Harris, aged 37, described her work to the Mines Commission in 1842 in these words:

"I was married at 23, and went into a colliery when I was married . . .

Women in the mines

"I have a belt round my waist, and a chain passing between my legs, and I go on my hands and feet. The road is very steep, and we have to hold by a rope; and when there is no rope, by anything we can catch hold of. There are six women and about six boys and girls in the pit I work in. It is very hard work for a woman. The pit is very wet where I work, and the water comes over our clog-tops always, and I have seen it up to my thighs. It rains in at the roof terribly. My clothes are wet through almost all day long . . .

"My cousin looks after my children in the day time. I am very tired when I get home at night. I fall asleep sometimes before I get washed. I am not so strong as I was, and cannot stand my work so well as I used to. I have drawn till I have had the skin off me . . . My feller has beaten me many-a-time for not being ready. I were not used to it at first, and he had little patience."

Fanny Drake told the same Commission: "I have had to hurry up to the calves of my legs in water. It was as bad as this a fort-night at a time; and this was for half a year last winter. My feet were skinned, and just as if they were scalded, for the water was bad . . . I was off my work owing to it, and had a headache and bleeding at my nose."

Janet Duncan declared: "It is very severe work, especially when we have to stay before the tubs, on the brace, to prevent them coming down too fast; they frequently run too quick and knock us down; when they run over-fast we fly off the roads and let them go, or we should be crushed. Mary Peacock was severely crushed a fortnight since."

One pit foreman told the Commission that women often did harder and less pleasant tasks underground than the men: "Females submit to work in places where no man, or even lad, could be got to labour in. They work in bad roads, up to their knees in water, in a posture nearly double."

Mine Act (1842)

A Mines Act was passed in 1842 which banned women and girls from working below ground. Shortly afterwards a Scottish colliery manager reported: "We had about 100 females in our pits when the Act came into operation. Many of these have got work in brick fields and out-door labour from the farmers. Some have gone to service, one or two are married. Some are maintained by their relations, others earn a little by sewing."

Probably the most shocking of all women's employment was working in the coal mines. But as one overseer told a Parliamentary Commission, they were better workers than men as they did what they were told

59

In 1844 the working hours of women in factories were restricted to twelve a day, and three years later, to a daily limit of ten. More factory legislation followed during the 1860s and 1870s, but though it steadily improved working conditions for many women, the end of the century saw many of them still doing arduous and dangerous tasks. In the West Midlands, for example, women worked in the chain and nail-making industries:

"Jane Smith, aged 14 years and 9 months, who points and helps to cut nails, began to work when she was about 13, works

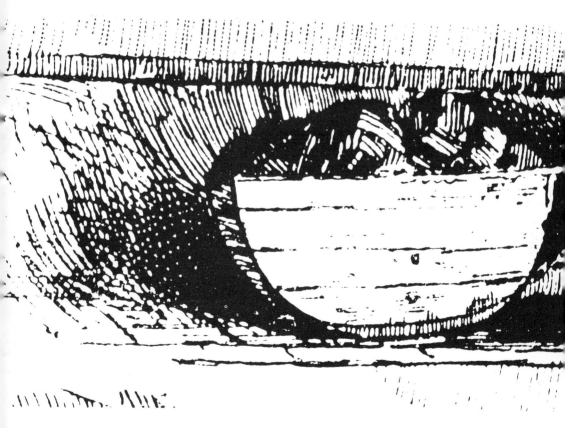

With a belt round her waist, and a chain between her legs, a woman could spend twelve hours each day bent double, dragging the coal tubs along the mine shafts

from 7 to 7, and is not strong enough for the work. A girl of eighteen stated that she worked twelve hours a day, and that her net earnings would be about 7s. 1d. *(35½p.)*. Sometimes she had bacon for her dinner; never fresh meat. She gave the weight of the heavier hammers she used at from 7 to 8 lbs, but Mr. Hoare who weighed them found they weighed 1 lb. and 2½ lb. respectively. It may be mentioned that the price of a dog chain which is made by these women for three farthings is, in London, from 1s. *(5p.)* to 1s. 3d. *(6p.)*. The value of the materials would be about

2d. *(1p.)."* (Select Committee on the Sweating System, *5th Report,* 1890).

Others, like Annie Harrison, were exposed to the dangers of lead poisoning:

"How old are you?"—"Twenty on the 28th of February last."

"Where have you been working?"—"At Bilston, at Messrs. Ralph & Jordan's"

"Are you working there now?"—"No, sir . . . I was very ill, obliged to leave. I had lead poison . . ."

"Did you find that the dust got down your throat much?"—"Yes sir, and it tastes very sweet, and I fetched it up off my stomach like that."

"Black?"—"Yes, in a large lump. If you have worked in the reds, it will come up red. If you have worked in the blues, it will come up blue. If you have worked in the blacks, it will come up black, and there is not one girl on the ground, if she will speak the truth, but will say it to you, and the yellow too." *(Report,* Departmental Committee on White Lead, 1893–94).

In 1888, the matchgirls at Bryant and May's East London factory went on strike. This was unprecedented for women so young and inexperienced. Annie Besant, a well-known socialist, helped to win them public support by describing their plight in her journal *The Link:* "The splendid salary of 4s. *(20p.)* is subject to deductions in the shape of fines . . . One girl was fined 1s. *(5p.)* for letting the web twist round a machine in the endeavour to save her fingers from being cut, and was sharply told to take care of the machine, 'never mind your fingers.' Another, who carried out the instructions and lost a finger thereby, was left unsupported while she was helpless. The wage covers the duty of submitting to an occasional blow from a foreman;—one, who appears to be a gentleman of variable temper—'clouts' them 'when he is mad'."

During the nineteenth century working-class women undertook many kinds of jobs in factories and workshops, though in any one district the opportunities open to them were probably very limited. Whatever job she chose, a woman could be sure that the work would be hard and tedious. Her continuing need was for shorter hours, higher wages, and safer working conditions.

Matchgirls on strike from their factory in the East End of London, 1888.
Their cause was quickly taken up by campaigners for women's rights.

Although she shared this need with her fellow male workers, there were times, as some of the above extracts show, when these men were directly responsible for making her lot more difficult. Added to this, her employer, of course, was nearly always a man.

5 New Roles Wanted

THE NINETEENTH CENTURY provided little hope for any Marriage stakes independent-minded woman of the upper or middle classes to earn her own living. Such training as most received was for one role only, that of wife. For young women marriage was the paramount goal in life, as shown by this letter of 1798 from a 23-year-old girl to the *Monthly Museum,* an early women's journal with an advice column:

"My papa and mama have been trying for the last three years to match me, and have for that purpose carried me from our country seat to London, from London to Brighton, from Brighton to Bath, and from Bath to Cheltenham, where I now am, backwards and forwards, till the family carriage is almost worn out, one of the horses is become blind and another lame, without my having more than a nibble, for I have never yet been able to hook my fish.

"I begin to be afraid that there is something wrong in their manner of baiting for a husband, or of mine of laying in the line to catch him . . . though I have . . . never acted the prude, but at every proper advance have looked as much as to say, 'Come on, if you dare.' I know not how it is, no one has ever offered me anything beyond a fashionable compliment."

The "Old Woman" who ran the advice feature replied: "Eagerness always defeats its own end, and sometimes is attended with the most fatal consequences to the unhappy woman who is the object of such indelicate and mischievous conduct . . . I think the parents of my lively correspondent are much more to blame for their impotency, than she is for her ill success . . . Jewels are not worn every day, nor should beauty be too much exposed to the vulgar eye . . . men will ever be more enamoured of the flower which they have found in the shade."

The Victorians created what has been called "the Feminine Illusion", glorifying the purity of Womanhood and endowing the perfect wife and mother with qualities which were near divine. One Victorian journal claimed that Woman was "given to man as his better angel, to dissuade him from vice, to stimulate him to virtue, to make home delightful and life joyous . . . In the exercise of these gentle and holy charities, she fulfils her high vocation. But great as is the influence of the maiden and wife, it seems to fade away when placed by that of the mother. It is the mother who is to make the citizens for earth . . . and happy are they who thus fulfil the sacred and dignified vocation allotted to them by Providence."

This was no good to the middle-class woman who wanted to make a career. Elsewhere in the same periodical the Editor declared: "Let man take his claimed supremacy . . . To woman will still remain a goodly heritage of which neither force nor competition can deprive her. The heart is her domain, and there she is an empress . . . To watch over the few dear objects of regard with an eye that never sleeps, and a care that cannot change: to think, to act, to suffer, to sacrifice, to live, to die for them, their happiness, their assured safety—these constitute Woman's true triumph . . . her love sustained by highest Genius." *(The Ladies Cabinet,* 1847).

Spinsters

What of the unmarried woman in this class, who might become homeless on the death of her parents? Not only was she ill-prepared to earn a living, but the range of possible jobs was severely limited. Factory work or domestic service was socially beneath her. For many dressmaking or millinery was the only choice. So it appeared to be to Kate Nickleby.

"Ralph paused for a few moments, and seeing that he had now made pretty sure of the mother in case the daughter objected to his proposition, went on to say:

" 'The situation that I have made interest to procure, ma'am is with—with a milliner and dressmaker, in short.'

" 'A milliner!' cried Mrs. Nickleby.

" 'A milliner and dressmaker, ma'am,' replied Ralph. 'Dressmakers in London, as I need not remind you, ma'am, who are so well acquainted with all matters in the ordinary routine of life, make large fortunes, keep equipages, and, become persons of great wealth and fortune'."

Kate, however, found the work less attractive than her uncle had pictured it to Mrs. Nickleby:

"She [Kate] was awkward—her hands were cold—dirty—coarse—she could do nothing right; they [the customers] wondered how Madame Mantalini could have such people about her: requested they might see some other young woman the next time they came . . .

"Kate shed many bitter tears when these people were gone, and felt, for the first time, humbled by her occupation. She had, it is true, quailed at the prospect of drudgery and hard service; but she had felt no degradation in working for her bread, until she found herself exposed to insolence and the coarsest pride." (Charles Dickens, *Nicholas Nickleby*, 1839).

Twenty-five years after Dickens told of Kate's experiences, a Mr. Isaacson, of Madame Elise's Dressmaking and Millinery Establishment, Regent Street, London, told a Government Commission: "We have from 70 to 80 residents and about 25 day-workers in the season. We do everything we can to make those who live with us comfortable and to keep them respectable . . . We pay £100 a year to a physician, that they may be attended free of cost. He calls every day, and the housekeeper informs him if any one is ill . . .

"Letters come with coronets and elaborate monograms for the young ladies. Such things have but one meaning, and commonly but one end." (Children's Employment Commission, *Second Report*, 1864).

Another Report, issued about the same time, stated: "Milliners and dressmakers, as far as regards social position, may be conveniently classed together . . . It is difficult to estimate their numbers correctly, but it may be stated that the names of 1750 dressmaking houses are mentioned in the Post Office London Directory, and that, giving an average of ten workers to each, the number 17,500 is obtained." (The Sanitary Circumstances of

Dressmaking and millinery were among the few occupations open to middle class women without other means of support. At best, it was a precarious way of making a living

Dressmakers and other Needlewomen in London: *Sixth Report of Medical Officer of the Privy Council,* 1863).

Prostitution   Throughout the 1800s prostitution was a major social problem, especially in the large towns. Most prostitutes came from the poor, but some had middle class origins:

"Thousands of young females of respectable parents who have been discreetly brought up and educated, and who are therefore

An illustration from a fashion journal, 1857. Such elaborate fashions were only possible because large numbers of dressmakers and seamstresses provided the necessary cheap labour.

unfitted for the drudgery of common service, are necessitated by the pecuniary misfortunes of their parents to earn a livelihood by needlework. All other female occupations equally suitable for them, or of a superior kind, require comparatively few individuals to supply them. It is notorious that such is the rivalship amongst females in this business, that employment is generally exceedingly precarious, and the profit very small.

"Many of such young ladies having in vain sought for a slender pittance, their parents being either dead, or through misfortunes unable to provide for them, therefore without a home and pressed by poverty, in a moment of despair resort to prostitution and its concomitants—misery, disease and death! The police reports of the Metropolis show that many young prostituted females from the polish of their manners, and from the history they relate, must have had a respectable origin: and that they have become a prey to this vice through their inability to procure an employment suited to their capacities, and through the impulses of sheer want. Hence the great extent of prostitution." *(Pamphleteer,* 1827).

Governesses   The most promising career open to a middleclass woman was to become a governess, though even here conditions might be far from easy. It was the road which Jane Eyre decided to explore in order to escape from Lowood School:

"I sat up in bed . . . and then I proceeded to think again with all my might. What do I want? A new place, in a new house amongst new faces, under new circumstances; I want this because it is of no use wanting anything better. How do people do to get a new place? They apply to friends, I suppose. I have no friends. There are many others who have no friends, who must look about for themselves and be their own helpers; and what is their resource? . . .

"Feverish with vain labour, I got up and took a turn in the room; undrew the curtain, noted a star or two, shivered with cold, and again crept to bed.

"A kind fairy, in my absence, had surely dropped the required suggestion on my pillow, for as I lay down it came quietly and naturally to my mind: Those who want situations advertise; you must advertise in the *—shire Herald.*

"With earliest day, I was up: I had my advertisement written, enclosed, and directed before the bell rang to rouse the school. It ran thus:

" 'A young lady accustomed to tuition' (had I not been a teacher for two years?) 'is desirous of meeting with a situation in a private family where the children are under fourteen' (I thought that as I was barely eighteen, it would not do to undertake the guidance of pupils nearer my own age). 'She is qualified to teach the usual branches of a good English education, together with French, Drawing, and Music . . . Address J. E., Post Office, Lowton, —shire'."

Some days later Jane received this letter in answer to her advertisement:

" 'If J.E., who advertised in the —*shire Herald* of last Thursday, possesses the acquirements mentioned; and if she is in a position to give satisfactory references as to character and competency: a situation can be offered here where the salary is thirty pounds per annum. J.E. is requested to send references, name, address, and all particulars to the direction: Mrs. Fairfax, Thornfield, near Millcote, —shire'." (Charlotte Brontë, *Jane Eyre,* 1847).

In William Thackeray's *Vanity Fair* (1847), Miss Pinkerton, who ran a school for young ladies at The Mall, Chiswick, was asked to find a governess to work for Lady Fuddleston. She suggested two candidates:

Vanity Fair

"Either of these young ladies is perfectly qualified to instruct in Greek, Latin, and the rudiments of Hebrew; in mathematics and history, in Spanish, French, Italian, and geography; in music, vocal and instrumental; in dancing, without the aid of a master; and in the elements of natural sciences.

"In the use of the globes both are proficient. In addition to these, Miss Tuffin . . . can instruct in the Syriac language, and the elements of Constitutional law. But as she is only eighteen years of age, and of exceedingly pleasing personal appearance, perhaps this young lady may be objectionable in Sir Huddleston Fuddleston's family.

"Miss Letitia Hawky, on the other hand, is not personally well-favoured. She is twenty-nine; her face is much pitted with the smallpox. She has a halt in her gait, red hair, and a trifling obliquity of vision. Both ladies are endowed with every moral and religious virtue."

A governess had to know something about many subjects. Charlotte Brontë protested in a letter to a friend: "It is both absurd and cruel to attempt to raise still higher the standard of acquirements. Already governesses are not half or a quarter paid for what they teach, nor in most instances is half or a quarter of their attainments required by their pupils.

"It is more physical and mental strength, denser moral impassability that they require, rather than additional skill in arts or sciences.

"It is true the world requires a brilliant list of accomplishments. For £20 per annum it expects in one woman the attainments of several professors—but the demand is insensate, and I think should rather be resisted than complied with."

Being a governess was not well paid. There could be long periods out of work. In 1841, about the time that Charlotte wrote the above words, a Governesses' Benevolent Institution was set up to afford "assistance privately and delicately to ladies in temporary distress."

Florence Nightingale

The professions were closed to women. In a little-known essay, *Cassandra*, Florence Nightingale commented: "Women often long to enter some man's profession where they would find direction, competition (or rather opportunity of measuring the intellect with others) and, above all, time.

"Women are never supposed to have any occupation of sufficient importance NOT to be interrupted, except 'suckling their fools', and women themselves have accepted this, have written books to support it and have trained themselves to consider whatever they do as NOT of such value to the world or to others as the first 'claim of social life'. They have accustomed themselves to consider intellectual occupation as merely a selfish amusement, which it is their 'duty' to give up to every trifler more selfish than themselves."

The frustration felt by one woman forced to lead an idle life is shown in Charlotte Brontë's novel *Shirley* (1849):

" 'Caroline,' demanded Miss Keeldar, abruptly, 'don't you wish you had a profession—a trade?'

" 'I wish it fifty times a day. As it is, I often wonder what I came into the world for. I long to have something absorbing and compulsory to fill my head and hands, and to occupy my thoughts'."

Male opposition in the professions

When women did try to enter professions or trades formerly reserved for men, they met with fierce opposition: "Mr. Bennett (of Cheapside, London), who has laboured so earnestly to open the manufacture of watches to women, told us an anecdote the other day which illustrates at once the difficulties women have to contend with (from the other sex, we are sorry to say), in making their way into a sphere of labour hitherto considered sacred to the men, and the success that attended their courageous efforts.

"Three young ladies, after a preliminary training at the Marlborough House School of Design, applied to him for occupation in engraving the backs of gold watches. Although perfect strangers to this kind of work, in six months, he tells us, they became as practised artists as a mere apprentice would have been in six years. At the end of this time, when they were making each three pounds a week by their labour, the men in the shop struck. These 'foreigners', as they were termed, must go, or *they* would; and Mr. Bennett was obliged, sadly against his will, to comply with their wishes." (Andrew Wynter, *Our Social Bees*, 1869).

Florence Nightingale was determined to make nursing a /*Nursing* trained profession open to women of all classes. Her success can be gauged from the following, written in 1896: "In no walk of life has the desire of certain women for independence and usefulness outside their homes found on the whole a more satisfactory expression than in the adoption of the profession of hospital nurse. The census at each decade shows an increase in the numbers of women so employed.

"All classes are drawn upon to satisfy the demand. Many are ladies by birth and education and many belong to the upper servant class. Daughters of clergymen, military and naval officers, of doctors, of farmers, of tradesmen and artisans are found side by side in all the great metropolitan hospitals . . .

"Great numbers apply every year to be taken on as nurses. One matron told us that last year she had 2,500 applications. Candidates must as a rule be not less than twenty-three years of age, and have special qualifications. Among other things stated on the printed papers usually given to them it is not uncommon to read, 'You are required to be punctual, quiet and orderly, cleanly and neat, methodical and active, patient, cheerful, and kindly, careful and trustworthy'." (Charles Booth, *Life and Labour of the People in London*, 1896).

Although acceptable as nurses, women were not considered *Women doctors*

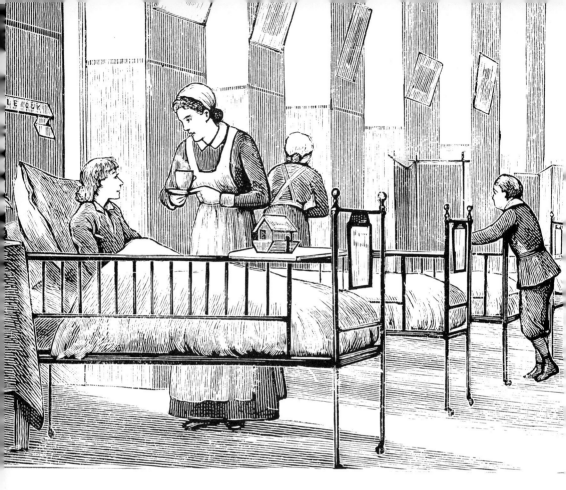

fit to train as doctors: "Can we deny that the general delicacy of females is a serious bar to an occupation which necessitates exposure at all hours and in all weather? Are there not physical qualifications which are insurmountable?" ("Physician of Twenty-one Years Standing", in *The English Woman's Journal,* 1862).

All manner of obstacles were put in the way of women becoming doctors. When, in 1859, Elizabeth Blackwell became the first to be registered in Britain, having obtained a medical degree in the United States, it was at once decided to disallow any further registration of those who held only foreign medical qualifications. A few years later Elizabeth Garrett, unable to attend any of the

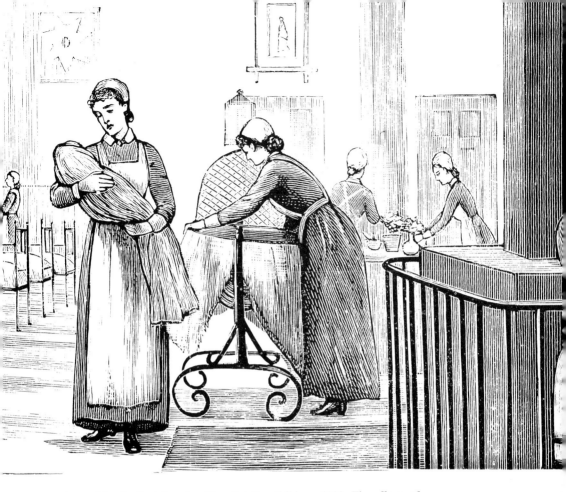

A ward in the East London Hospital for Children, 1883. The efforts of
Florence Nightingale had opened another career to women, that of nursing

country's medical schools, found that if she passed the examination of the Society of Apothecaries her name would have to be
placed on the Medical Register. Her success led the Society to
stop any more women entering the profession by this route.

In 1870 there was new evidence of discrimination. At Edinburgh, a small group of women, intent on becoming doctors, was
being allowed to sit some of the University's examinations.
Although one of the group, Mary Peachey, came top in the
chemistry examination, she was denied the scholarship usually
awarded to the candidate with the highest marks. The University's action brought sharp attacks from *The Times* and the
Lancet, as well as this rebuke from *Punch:*

"Whatever we may think of the ladies' claims to Electoral privileges, there can be no question as to their full right to the spoils of victory when they face our selfish sex in fair fight, and beat us.

"This, Miss MARY EDITH PEACHEY has done at Edinburgh, coming out as one of the first four students of chemistry, and as such claiming one of the Hope Scholarships.

"This claim Dr. Crum Brown resists on the ground that the lady-students at Edinburgh, being taught in separate courses and classes, are not 'students' in the sense that entitles them to the money-prizes of the University.

"And yet Miss PEACHEY has been awarded one of the five medals given to the five highest students of the Session!

"The University Senate has confirmed Dr. Crum Brown's decision.

"Titus Salt, Jun., of Saltaire, very fairly, as it seems to *Punch*, protests against this in *The Times*, and asks those of his fellow-men who feel that an injustice has been done to a woman by our sex, to help him raise a fund to support Miss PEACHEY through her curriculum, as the income of the Hope Scholarship would have done.

"Bread and salt *ought* to go together; but in this conflict of opinion between CRUM and SALT, *Mr. Punch* votes with SALT." (23rd April, 1870).

Although Parliament decided in 1876 that universities could, if they wished, accept women as medical students, it was a long time before many were persuaded to do so.

6 *The Right to be Educated*

SO LONG as the law allowed children to be employed in factory, field or mine, few boys or girls from poor families received any education. A number of private schools for such children did exist, but they were of a very low standard:

"There is a school in the court, attended by about fifty scholars, held in a room twelve feet square, and eight and a half feet high, which is the sole dwelling of the schoolmaster, his wife and six children. The unwholesome condition of the air under these circumstances may be easily conceived.

"The mode of payment to the teacher of this school is remarkable and characteristic. A kind of club, which does not consist exclusively of the parents of the scholars, meets every Saturday evening at a public-house. When, after some hours spent in drinking and smoking, a subscription is raised, and handed over to the schoolmaster, who forms one of the company, and who is expected to spend a part of the money in regaling the subscribers." (G. R. Porter in an article published by the Central Society of Education, 1837).

More important to working-class children were the schools of two religious societies, the National Society founded by Anglicans, and the British and Foreign Society run by Nonconformists, both founded early in the nineteenth century. In 1839 Lord John Russell announced that Queen Victoria "has observed with deep concern the want of instruction which is still observable among the poorer classes of Her subjects. All the inquiries show a deficiency in the general Education of the People which is not in accordance with the character of a Civilized and Christian Nation...

Religious schools

Above Education was slow to reach the children of poor families. A ragged school in Edinburgh, photographed in 1857

Below A class of schoolgirls being drilled in 1905. Discipline was very strict and obedience had to be complete

"It is some consolation to Her Majesty to perceive that of late years the zeal for popular education has increased, that the Established Church has made great efforts to promote the building of schools, and that the National and British and Foreign School Societies have actively endeavoured to stimulate the liberality of the benevolent and enlightened friends of general Education."

That same year a Committee of the Privy Council was set up to supervise the spending of government grants to the two societies, with school inspectors acting as servants of the new body. The main aim of educating the poor was to produce hard-working and law-abiding citizens:

"Their Lordships are strongly of opinion that no plan of education ought to be encouraged in which intellectual instruction is not subordinate to the regulation of the thought and habits of the children by the doctrines and precepts of revealed religion."

Boys and girls were to be regimented: "Before a teacher commences a lesson, he should drill the children into good order. Amongst other things they should be commanded to sit upright, or to sit exactly in front of their desks, or to place their feet in a proper position, or to sit at a proper distance from each other, or to place their books or slates properly—and so on. They should be marched in and out of their classes in regular military order." (*Educational Expositor*, October, 1854).

The Education Act of 1870 aimed at covering England and Wales with "good schools". Where such schools did not exist— and there were many areas—elected School Boards were established to "fill the gaps". Each School Board was given the power to enforce attendance within its own district, but another ten years were to pass before there was a national system of compulsory elementary education. Rather surprisingly, this compulsion was directed at girls as well as boys:

Education Act (1870)

"Among the public buildings of the Metropolis the London Board Schools occupy a conspicuous place . . . Taken as a whole, they may be said fairly to represent the high-water mark of the public conscience in its relation to the education of the children of the people.

"A Board School is commonly arranged in three storeys,

corresponding to the three departments, boys, girls, and infants, each storey having an entrance and playground of its own . . .

"In the girls' department . . . Everywhere we are met by tokens of penury and bad conditions at home. Children are pointed out to us stunted in growth, with faces old beyond their years, burdened out of school with the whole charge of the wretched little home. 'Never no time to play,' as one of them explains . . . Even the youngest of these girls, we find, has often to wash and dress and feed the baby, cook the father's dinner when the mother is at work, and 'clean up' the single room in which the family live.

Cookery lessons

"One step in advance, however, has recently been taken. In every London Board School the older girls learn cookery. A fair number of the children have been to the cookery centre. All are fond of it. Their faces brighten the moment it is spoken of. Some of them, the tidier ones with decent mothers, are proud to tell that they have made at home the things they learned at the classes. Shepherd's pie, rock cakes, and Irish stew, seem popular attempts. All declare that their dish turned out well; with the addition, usually, that 'father ate it'.

"Many things are taught at these cookery centres besides cookery—cleanliness, neatness, precision, despatch. The observing faculties are brought into play, the latent womanliness developed. All these girls get to something that they can understand and be interested in, and which works into their scheme of life." Booth, *Life and Labour*, c. 1897).

Boys and girls alike resented having to attend school. Truancy became a serious problem. Teachers, faced with classes of unwilling pupils, often resorted to the use of the cane *(The Schoolmaster,* 1884):

> *Solomon said, in accents mild,*
> *Spare the rod and spoil the child;*
> *Be they man or be they maid,*
> *Whack 'em and wallop 'em, Solomon said.*

Most working-class parents remained unconvinced of the need for girls to be educated. But most middle-class parents took steps to provide some schooling for their daughters, even if only to teach certain social skills and graces. For those who championed the cause of women's rights, however, education was seen as a powerful weapon in the struggle to win political and economic equality.

As early as 1753 Lady Mary Wortley Montagu had expressed ideas about the education of girls, in several letters to her daughter giving advice on the schooling of her grand-daughters: *Lady Montagu*

"Dear Child, You have given me a great deal of satisfaction by your account of your eldest daughter. I am particularly pleased to hear she is a good arithmetician; it is the best proof of understanding: the knowledge of numbers is one of the chief distinctions between us and brutes . . .

"The use of knowledge in our sex, beside the amusement of solitude, is to moderate the passions, and learn to be contented with a small expense, which are the certain effects of a studious life; and it may be preferable even to that fame which men have engrossed to themselves, and will not suffer us to share."

Some middle class girls, like the young Helen in *Miss Miminy-Piminy* (1860), went to private schools sometimes little better *A Victorian girl at school*

The Royal Masonic Institution for Girls, at Battersea-rise, London, in 1875

than the establishments attended by the poor. Annie Keary, who wrote this story, was probably recalling her first school:

"I will tell you exactly what the school-room was like, and what Helen did there. It was a large room without any carpet on the floor, and with forms placed in rows across it. There were two Miss Staintons. One sat at the top and the other at the bottom of the room. They were properly called Miss Stainton and Miss Anne Stainton; but little Helen never called them so — she always called them the cross Miss Stainton and the pretty Miss Stainton. The cross Miss Stainton sat at the top of the room, near the fireplace. Over her head there hung a long piece of cardboard bound with black ribbon, and on it was written every Monday morning the names of all the girls who had been naughty during the past week. That piece of cardboard was called *the bad list*. The pretty Miss Stainton sat at the bottom of the room near the bay window that looked into the back garden. Over her head there hung another piece of cardboard bound with pink ribbon. It was *the good list,* and there were written the names of all the girls who had been very good during the week."

Other girls were educated at home, either being taught by governesses or, as in the case of the unfortunate Mary Butt (1775–1851), later to be Mrs. Sherwood, a well-known writer of children's books, by their parents. She wrote in her *Memoirs* (1854):

Iron collars   "It was the fashion then for children to wear iron collars round the neck, with blackboards strapped over the shoulders. To one of these I was subjected from my sixth to my thirteenth year. I generally did all my lessons standing in stocks, with this same collar round my neck; it was put on in the morning, and seldom taken off till late in the evening; and it was Latin which I had to study . . .!

"Though I was educated under the same roof till my brother was nine or ten years old, we were by no means subjected to the same management. I have described the discipline to which I was subjected, and for which I have many times thanked my God and my beloved mother, but a very different process was going on with my brother all this time, till he was sent to school. Whilst I was with my mother in her dressing-room, he was with my father

82

in his study, and no authority being used, he made such small progress in his Latin that it was suggested that I should be made to learn Latin with him; and my dear mother, in order that by her regularity she might make up for the intermitting habits of my father, set herself to learn Latin and thus became our tutor. Still, as she constantly obliged me to do my lessons, while no such authority was exercised over my brother when out of her sight, it proved that I soon got before him."

Emily Shore (1819–39) showed an even greater zest for learning which may well have contributed to her early death: "In looking back on the beginning of my illness, I feel sure that one of the principal causes of it was overworking my mind with too hard study, which is no uncommon cause of consumption. For many months before I was actually ill, I tasked my intellectual powers to the utmost. My mind never relaxed, never unbent; even in those hours meant for relaxation, I was still engaged in acquiring knowledge and storing my memory.

"While dressing, I learnt by heart chapters of the Bible, and repeated them when I walked out, and when I lay in bed; I read Gibbon when I curled my hair at night; at meals my mind was still bent on its improvement, and turned to arithmetic, history, and geography. This system I pursued voluntarily with the most unwearied assiduity, disregarding the increasing delicacy of my health, and the symptoms that it was giving way." *(Journal,* 18th September, 1837).

The Schools Inquiry Commission (1868) was greatly concerned *The Misses Buss* about the lack of secondary education for girls. While hundreds *and Beale* of public and grammar schools existed for boys, there were few for the opposite sex, and these were generally inferior. Two women who gave evidence before the Commission had already begun to improve the position for girls: these were Frances Buss, who had founded the North London Collegiate School in 1850, and Dorothea Beale, who became Head of the Cheltenham Ladies' College in 1858. Their example paved the way for the establishment of the Girls' Public Day School Company, which had built, by the end of the century, thirty-three schools, catering for over 7,000 girls.

The *Saturday Review* was particularly hostile towards the *Plague of women*

Members of Cambridge University demonstrating against the admission
of women, *c.* 1880

education of girls. In 1869 it declared, "A learned, or even an over-accomplished young woman, is one of the most intolerable monsters in creation." On another occasion it asked: "Is there a plague of Egypt worse than the strong-minded woman? However, we do not fear that this species of vermin will ever infest English drawing-rooms."

Emily Davies (1830–1921) was the sort of person that the *Saturday Review* despised. She wrote: "On all sides there is evidence that as regards intelligence and good sense, English women of the middle classes are held in small esteem. 'A woman's reason' means, in popular phrase, no reason at all. A man who lets it be known that he consults his wife endangers his own reputation for sense. A habit of exaggeration, closely verging upon untruthfulness, is a recognized feminine characteristic. Newspaper writers, expressing the prevailing sentiment, assume towards women an indulgent air which is far from flattering, giving them credit for good intentions, but very little capacity." *(On Secondary Instruction Relating to Girls,* 1864).

*Emily Davies*

If women were to prove this view false, Emily Davies believed, they needed education. She particularly wanted to see higher education, and campaigned against the ban on women sitting university examinations. In 1869 she opened a school for women students at Hitchin, Hertfordshire. It moved to Cambridge in 1874 to become Girton College. Shortly afterwards a second women's college, Newnham Hall, was established in that city, while at Oxford, Somerville College and Lady Margaret Hall were opened in 1879 and 1883. *Punch* commented in 1884 on these developments in characteristic style:

The Woman of the Future! She'll be deeply read, that's certain,
With all the education gained at Newnham or at Girton;
She'll puzzle men in Algebra with horrible quadratics,
Dynamics, and the mysteries of higher mathematics;
Or, if she turns to classic tomes a literary roamer,
She'll give you bits of HORACE *or sonorous lines from* HOMER.

*The educated woman*

You take a maiden in to dine, and find, with consternation,
She scorns the light frivolities of modern conversation;

And not for her the latest bit of fashionable chatter,
Her pretty head is well-nigh full of more important matter;

You talk of Drama or Burlesque, theatric themes pursuing
She only thinks of what the Dons at Oxford may be doing.

A female controversialist will tackle you quite gaily,
With scraps from Pearson on the Creed, *or extracts culled from*
    Paley;
And, if you parry these homethrusts just like a wary fencer,
She'll floor you with some STUART MILL, *or else with* HERBERT
    SPENCER.
In fact, unless with all such lore you happen to be laden,
You'd better shun, if you've a chance, an educated maiden.

The Woman of the Future may be very learned-looking,
But dare we ask if she'll know aught of housekeeping or cooking;
She'll read far more, and that is well, than empty-headed beauties,
But has she studied with it all a woman's chiefest duties?
We wot she'll ne'er acknowledge, till her heated brain grows cooler,
That Woman, not the Irishman, should be the true home-ruler.

O pedants of these later days, why go on undiscerning,
To overload a woman's brain and cram our girls with learning,
You'll make a woman half a man, the souls of parents vexing,
To find that all the gentle sex this process is unsexing.
Leave one or two nice girls before the sex your system smothers,
Or what on earth will poor men do for sweethearts, wives, and
    mothers?'

London University opened its degrees to women in 1878. Oxford and Cambridge proved much more difficult for women to conquer. Whilst both allowed women to sit their degree examinations, they long remained unwilling actually to give them degrees. Oxford did not relent until 1920, and Cambridge not until after the Second World War.

7 "Two Heads Are Better Than One!"

RAY STRACHEY, in his book about the women's movement, tells of an exchange which is supposed to have taken place between Elizabeth Garrett and Emily Davies. "Well, Elizabeth," the forceful Emily said, "It's quite clear what has to be done. I must devote myself to securing higher education, while you open the medical profession to women. After these things are done, we must see about getting the vote." *(The Cause,* 1928).

Amongst those who played a prominent part in the ensuing struggle to gain women the vote were Millicent Fawcett (1847–1929), a younger sister of Elizabeth Garrett, and Lydia Becker (1827–90). Through committees in Manchester, London, Bristol and Edinburgh these women, and others like them, tried to rally support for the cause of women's suffrage in the period following the Reform Act of 1867.

Lydia Becker founded and edited the *Women's Suffrage Journal*. After one public meeting she wrote to a friend: "How they listened—how they cheered. If my eyes had been shut I should have fancied it was men who were cheering and clapping ... I can't tell you how my heart went out to these women: and to see them look at me—oh, it was really sacred—awful: it was if I received a baptism. It has been a new life to me to know and feel the strength there is in those women."

At Lydia's death the *Pall Mall Gazette* said: "After bearing the heat and burden of the day, we wish Miss Becker could have lived to see the fruits of her labours." The *Birmingham Daily Post* proclaimed: "The labours of Miss Becker have changed the views of society."

Lydia Becker

Women soon made some political progress. In 1869 the right to vote in municipal elections was extended to them, while next year they became eligible to serve on the new School Boards. When Elizabeth Garrett, Lydia Becker and Emily Davies were elected to the first London School Board in 1871, the *Englishwoman's Review* was delighted: "It removes in some degree the stigma of inferiority hitherto attached to women."

But the chance to take part in Parliamentary elections continued to elude women. In 1870 the first separate Women's Suffrage Bill, which was drafted by Richard Pankhurst, was defeated, largely due to the opposition of the Liberal Prime Minister, William Gladstone. Later attempts to get such a Bill through Parliament proved no more successful. On one occasion, an M.P. stated that if the measure was passed, "husbands would find only dry metaphysical lectures awaiting them instead of their dinners, and advised English women to rely upon their natural attractions and their domestic virtues, and upon the proud intellectual position which some of their sex had attained." (*Englishwoman's Review*, 1872).

"This mad wicked folly" Queen Victoria was disgusted by women who clamoured for rights. When she learned that Lady Amberley, the daughter-in-law of Lord John Russell, a former Prime Minister, had addressed a meeting in support of female suffrage, she wrote: "The Queen is most anxious to enlist everyone who can speak or write or join in checking this mad, wicked folly of 'Women's Rights' with all its attendant horrors, on which her poor feeble sex is bent, forgetting every sense of womanly feeling and propriety. Lady Amberley ought to get a *good whipping*."

The Queen's views were expressed here privately. Had they been made public, she would certainly have found many sympathisers amongst her subjects. It was generally believed in the 1870s, with some truth, that the advocates of women's emancipation represented very few of the female sex. A contributor to *The Englishwoman's Domestic Magazine* of 1870 commented: "That women as a body desire a vote in Parliament I do not think. The women who do have such a wish form but a very small proportion of those whose opinions they say they represent."

88

Mr. and Mrs. Gladstone. Unintentionally perhaps, the scene typifies Gladstone's attitude to women; whether she cooked his meals, bore his children or held a parasol for him, woman was man's servant

In 1884 a new Reform Bill, aimed at extending the male fran- chise still further, raised the hopes of those in the suffrage move- ment, for they believed that they could persuade Parliament to pass an amendment giving women the vote. But though 79 Liberal M.P.s indicated that they were in favour of such a step, Gladstone ensured that women would not be included in the Bill's provisions. Millicent Fawcett's husband, who was a member of the Government, was so angry at Gladstone's attitude that he refused to vote in support of the Bill, whereupon Gladstone sent a memorandum to him and two other rebels:

"It has probably come to the notice of my colleagues that, in a division early this morning, which was known to be vital to the Franchise Bill and to the Government, three of its members abstained from voting.

"Preliminary intimation had been given to this effect, and some effort had been made to bring about a different intention. This change of mind was hoped for, but no question of surprise can be raised.

"It is, however, an elementary rule, necessary for the cohesion and character of Administrations, that on certain questions, and notably on questions vital to their existence, their members should vote together. In the event of their not doing so their intention to quit the Government is presumed, and in all ordinary circum- stances ought to take effect."

But, Gladstone went on to explain, "ordinary circumstances" did not prevail. Therefore, being unwilling to jeopardise his Ministry, he requested Fawcett and the other rebels to remain in office. The same week *Punch* contained this verse "by a mis- ogynist":

> *O Woman! Suffrageless, you Shes*
> *Have made the world a Little-ease.*
> *But with a vote? Great* SCOTT! *I vow*
> *Our daily life would be* all *row!*

The women's movement received a bitter blow in 1889 when a manifesto entitled *An Appeal Against Female Suffrage* was published with the signatures of 104 women. It said that women

Opposite Queen Victoria and Prince Albert. Despite holding the most powerful position in the kingdom, the Queen strongly opposed rights for women

"strongly protest against the proposed parliamentary franchise to women," which was "distasteful to the great majority of women and mischievous both to themselves and the State." Mrs. Humphrey Ward, the novelist, who was amongst the signatories, later formed a Women's National Anti-Suffrage League.

N.U.W.S.S. In 1897 many suffrage committees and societies banded together to form the National Union of Women's Suffrage Societies, with Millicent Fawcett as president. It attacked the arguments of the anti-suffragists:

"Anti-Suffragists say that 'The Voter, in giving a vote, pledges himself to uphold the consequences of his vote at all costs,' and that 'women are physically incapable of making this pledge.' *What does this mean?*

"When the issue at a General Election is PEACE or WAR, and a man votes for WAR, does he himself have to fight? *No!!* The men who fight are seldom qualified to vote, and the men who vote are never compelled to fight.

"*What is the Voter's part in War?* He is called upon to PAY THE BILL.

"*Are Women physically incapable of this?* Apparently NOT. They are forced to pay in equal proportions with the men who alone have made the decision. Surely this is not fair! Since men and women are equally involved in the consequences, should not men and women equally have power to decide?

"'But some matters discussed in the House of Commons concern men more than women.' True, but just as many concern women more than men.

"Is not the Housing Problem a woman's question, since '*Woman's place is the home?*' Are not EDUCATION, a Pure Milk Supply, and a Children's Charter questions for women, since '*The Woman's business is to look after the baby?*' Is not the Taxation of Food a woman's question since women are '*The housekeepers* of the Nation?'

"Women claim *votes*, not because they are, or want to be, LIKE MEN, but because they are *Different*, and have somewhat different interests and different views. They want the vote as a tool, with which to do *not Men's Work*, but *Woman's Work*, which men have left undone, or are trying unsuccessfully to do.

THE A.S.S— "Woe and desolation! Behold a woman-enfranchised England, prostrate beneath her descending foes!"

A satirical cartoon showing what many feared would happen if women, who out-numbered men, were given the vote

IS THIS RIGHT?

THE OPEN
MARKET

Woman. Why can't I have an umbrella too?

Voter. You can't. You ought to stop at home.

Woman. Stop at home indeed! I have my Living to earn.

A postcard published in support of women's suffrage

"LET THE WOMEN HELP! *'Two Heads are Better than one!!'*"
(Handbill distributed by the National Union of Women's
Suffrage Societies).

By the end of the century, though still voteless, women had *Married*
improved their position in law. Two Married Women's Property *Women's*
Acts—1870 and 1882—had allowed a wife to own property and *Property Acts*
dispose of it as she wished. Legislation in 1886 gave a deserted
wife the right to sue her husband for maintenance. A contributor
to one women's magazine, at the time of the first Property Bill,
cautioned its readers against expecting too much from such legal
gains:

"It is absurd to think that because these rights are granted to
married women marriage is thence to be regarded as a sort of
partnership . . . Nothing could be more unfounded than the idea
that men should cease to be masters of their own households."
(*The Englishwoman's Domestic Magazine,* 1870).

Feminism was not confined to Britain. Throughout the nine- *American*
teenth century a similar movement had been developing in the *women*
United States. In 1848, at Seneca Falls, New York, a women's
conference declared:

"The history of mankind is a history of repeated injuries and
usurpations on the part of man toward woman, having in direct
object the establishment of an absolute tyranny over her. To
prove this, let facts be submitted to a candid world.

"He has never permitted her to exercise her inalienable right
to the elective franchise.

"He has compelled her to submit to laws, in the formation of
which she had no voice.

"He has withheld from her rights which are given to the most
ignorant and degraded men—both natives and foreigners.

"Having deprived her of this first right of a citizen, the elective
franchise, thereby leaving her without representation in the halls
of legislation, he has oppressed her on all sides.

"He has made her, if married, in the eye of the law, civilly dead.

"He has taken from her all right in property, even to the wages
she earns . . .

"He has denied her the facilities for obtaining a thorough
education, all colleges being closed against her.

Another propaganda postcard for women's suffrage

"He allows her in Church, as well as State, but a subordinate position, claiming Apostolic authority for her exclusion from the ministry, and, with some exceptions, from any public participation in the affairs of the Church.

"He has created a false public sentiment by giving to the world a different code of morals for men and women, by which moral delinquencies which exclude women from society, are not only tolerated, but deemed of little account in man."

After the American Civil War, some American women believed that they were now worse off than former male slaves:

"Slavery is not yet abolished in the United States. It is the boast of our republic that it is a nation of free men; it points triumphantly to its last great act, the emancipation of four millions of negroes, and forgets, in its pride and self-gratulation, that within its boundaries are still left at least ten millions of bond-women, who have no voice in the government, and no rights, except such as their masters have chosen to give them.

"That the women in the United States are many of them comfortable and happy, as they are, is no argument in favour of the system of government under which they live . . .

"In the interests of the race it is most important that women should be roused to a sense of their subject condition, and to the humiliation which it involves. They should no longer accept the ideal of womanly character which society offers them, but rise to the conception of the free and independent being that God intended a true woman to be. They should no longer tamely submit to the bondage in which custom and education have for ages held them, but break off the shackles which bind them. They should demand a freedom of thought and a freedom of action equal to that which man demands for himself, and which God designed as the true means for the development of both sexes.

"The enfranchisement of woman is the germ from which shall spring the reorganization of society." (Laura Curtis Bullard, *The Slave-Women of America*, 1870).

By 1900 women in a few American states had won the vote. But they were to wait another twenty years before being given the same right in federal elections.

8 Militant Suffragettes

MOST WOMEN campaigning for the vote were "constitutionalists" —they wished to use only orderly means to achieve their ends. A growing number of women, however, disappointed by the failure of such methods, became convinced that a more violent approach was needed. Amongst the leaders of these militants, christened "suffragettes" by the *Daily Mail,* were Emmeline Pankhurst (1858–1928), widow of Richard Pankhurst, and her daughters Christabel (1880–1958), Sylvia (1882–1960) and Adela (1885–1961). In October 1903, Mrs. Pankhurst founded the Women's Social and Political Union.

For many years the women's suffrage movement was handicapped by rivalry between the National Union and the W.S.P.U. Attempts to reconcile their differences failed. Some years later Christabel Pankhurst wrote: "If Mrs Fawcett and Mother had stood together at the door of the House of Commons, it might have opened. The Prime Minister could not easily have fought both wings of the Women's Movement." (Christabel Pankhurst, *Unshackled,* 1959).

Millicent Fawcett refused to join forces with the new suffragette organization. She remarked: "There are great and obvious advantages in unity, but I think we should not forget that there may be disadvantages too. The most striking example of unity which I know is that of the Gadarene swine, of whom it is recorded that they 'ran violently down a steep place to the sea, and perished in the waters'."

Although opposed to violence, Millicent could understand the frustration felt by the militants. In a letter to Lady Cavendish, *Women on the warpath*

Opposite Mrs. Emmeline Pankhurst being carried away after her arrest outside Buckingham Palace in May 1914

100

A suffragettes' meeting at Queen's Hall, London

Mrs. Fawcett wrote: "Militancy is abhorred by me, and the majority of suffragists. None of the great triumphs of the women's movement . . . have been won by physical force: they have been triumphs of moral and spiritual force. But militancy has been brought into existence by the blind blundering of politicians who have not understood the women's movement. I cannot wonder that people of excitable temperament have been goaded almost to madness by the 'shuffling and delay' with which our question has been treated in Parliament. If men had been treated by the House of Commons as women have been treated, there would have been bloody reprisals all over the country. I do say most deliberately and with the utmost conviction that what is called militancy is 'political unrest' caused by mishandling and misunderstanding by politicians of one of the greatest movements in the history of the world."

Cuts and bruises

The suffragettes soon began to make a public nuisance of themselves. In her autobiography Emmeline Pankhurst said: "We attended every meeting addressed by Mr. Churchill. We heckled him unmercifully; we spoiled his best points by flinging back such obvious retorts that the crowds roared with laughter . . . We questioned Mr. Asquith in Sheffield, Mr. Lloyd-George in Altrincham, Cheshire, the Prime Minister again in Glasgow, and we interrupted a great many other meetings as well. Always we were violently thrown out and insulted. Often we were painfully bruised and hurt." (Emmeline Pankhurst, *My Own Story,* 1914).

In a letter to Mrs. Fawcett written in June, 1909, Lady Frances Balfour described a meeting she had attended: "I am just back from a night with the militants. Lady Betty and I went to the Caxton Hall first. The speeches were of a very serious nature, almost like a service of dedication. There was no excitement. We were all asked not to move as the deputation left the Hall, to 'remain seated in silent thought for three minutes, and then to follow and cheer our comrades on in the Square.'

"The deputation consisted of nine, led by Mrs. Pankhurst . . . They all looked very high-strung and nervous. They passed out, their band marshalled on the stair to play them out. We followed some time after. The police in solid lines turned us into Victoria

Police arresting suffragettes who had chained themselves to the railings
outside Buckingham Palace in May 1914

Street. We slowly battled our way to the west side of Parliament Square and up to Whitehall; here we saw several arrests, the women all showing extraordinary courage in the rough rushes of the crowd round them. The crowd neither for us nor against, merely interested in it as a spectacle. The police kept us all moving, mounted men continually at work.

"We were finally driven up to the north end of Whitehall. B. and I stood on the Treasury steps watching the crowd slowly driven up by a wedge of police. The police on the pavement asked us to come down, and as we did so two women exactly in front of us threw stones at the windows. Poor shots; I don't think the glass was even cracked. A policeman flew on them, and had his arm round their necks before one could think. Crowd and police made a rush together, and B. and I were both knocked flat, falling in a rather ignominious heap! I was afraid the crowd would fall over on us, but we were quickly picked up and walled in by police and kept moving.

"The two women were swept away with incredible speed. The police naturally hustled rather more, and we got away by the Horse Guards. The courage that dares this handling I do admire. ... We saw one tall girl driven like a leaf up and down Whitehall ... There is a fine spirit, but whether it is not thrown away on these tactics remains a doubt in my mind. ... I wonder much what happened to them all. The ministerial *mot* was arrest and avoid charging them afterwards."

Courage of demonstrators Millicent Fawcett replied: "The physical courage of it all is intensely moving. It stirs people as nothing else can. I don't feel it is the right thing, and yet the spectacle of so much self-sacrifice moves people who would otherwise sit still and do nothing till the suffrage dropped into their mouths like ripe fruit . . . I am told that the reporters who actually see what takes place in the street are impressed; but they are not allowed to report things as they actually happened. What you tell me of 'a tall girl driven like a leaf up and down Whitehall' is a case in point. Nothing is reported except what can be turned into ridicule.

"Thank God you were not seriously hurt; but it is hateful to think of you being knocked down in a rowdy crowd. There is no doubt that the militant women are fighting this through in the

Hampstead Women's Social and Political Union,
178, FINCHLEY ROAD, N.W.

WINDOW BREAKING

AND

INCITEMENT

TO

MUTINY.

For Breaking Windows as a Political protest, Women are now in H.M. Gaols serving sentences of
Four and Six months imprisonment.

For Inciting Soldiers to Disobey Orders, a much more serious crime, known to the law as a felony, and punishable by penal servitude, the Publishers of the "Syndicalist," were sentenced to nine months hard labour, and the Printers of the paper to six months hard labour.

The Government under the pressure of men with votes reduced this sentence on the Publishers to
Six months imprisonment without hard labour,

and the sentence on the Printers to
One month without hard labour.

IS THIS JUSTICE TO
VOTELESS WOMEN ?

A handbill issued by the Hampstead branch of the Women's Social and Political Union. It condemned the sentences imposed after demonstrations in Downing Street

spirit of a religious revival movement. The more they are imprisoned and punished the more they go on."

Apart from breaking windows, the suffragettes raided Parliament and Downing Street, harried Ministers—sometimes
physically assaulting them—and forced the closure of the
National Gallery and the British Museum. *Punch* reported in
1913: "Underwriters at Lloyd's are now open to insure golf
courses against damage by Suffragettes. The premium is equivalent to 2 per cent, the rate being quoted for all eighteen holes at
£1 each for twelve months, underwriters to pay any claims for
damage to each green up to £50."

Death on Derby Day

Many suffragettes were sent to prison where they gained
further publicity for their cause by going on hunger strike. No
single event drew more attention to their activities than when, on
Derby Day 1913, Emily Davison threw herself under the King's
horse as it rounded Tattenham Corner and was killed. Another
suffragette, who was present at the race meeting, described what
happened to her shortly after this tragic incident occurred:

"There was an awful silence that seemed to go on for minutes;
then suddenly many cries and shouts arose as people swarmed
out on to the racecourse. I was rooted with horror until a man
snatched the paper I was holding in my hand (a copy of *The
Suffragette*) and beat it across my face."

Sex disease allegations

Fanaticism of the kind that led to the death of Emily Davison,
prompted some suffragettes to make the most outrageous of
statements. In 1913, for example, Christabel Pankhurst warned
women against marriage on the ridiculous grounds that 75 per
cent of the male population suffered from venereal disease:

"For severely practical, common-sensible, sanitary reasons,
women are chary of marriage. When the best-informed and most
experienced medical men say that the vast majority of men expose
themselves before marriage to sexual disease, and that only an
'insignificant minority,' as one authority puts it—25 per cent at
most—escape infection. When these medical authorities further
say that sexual disease is difficult, if not impossible, to cure,
healthy women naturally hesitate to marry.

"Mr. Punch's 'advice to those about to marry—Don't!' has a
true and terrible application to the facts of the case. 'Sacrifice

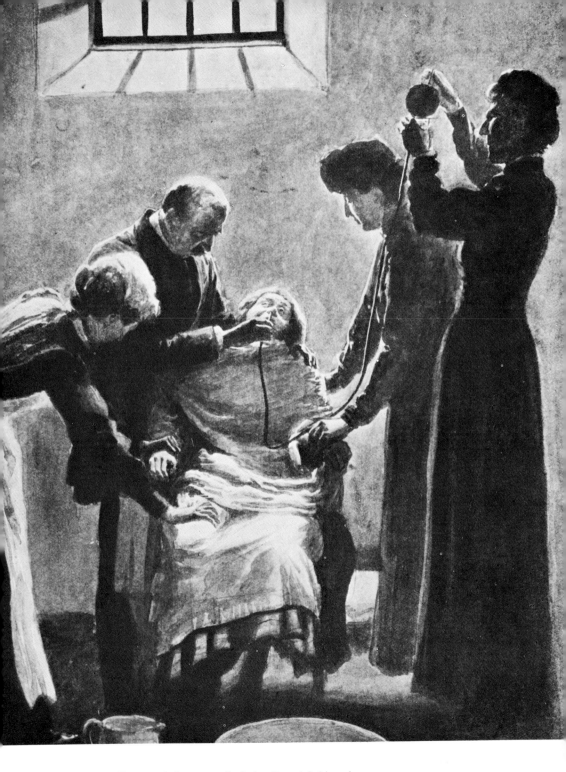

A suffragette on hunger strike being forced-fed in prison

yourself, sacrifice yourself,' is a cry that has lost its power over women . . . Now that women have learnt to think for themselves, . . . woman, in sacrificing herself, sacrifices the race." (Christabel Pankhurst, *The Great Scourge and How to End it*, 1913).

The opponents of women's suffrage could also overstate their case. Sir Almroth Wright declared: "The failure to recognise that man is the master, and why he is the master, lies at the root of the suffrage movement. By disregarding man's superior physical force, the power of compulsion upon which all government is based is disregarded. By leaving out of account those powers of the mind in which man is the superior, woman falls into the error of thinking that she can really compete with him, and that she belongs to the self-same intellectual caste. Finally, by putting out of sight man's superior money-earning capacity, the power of the purse is ignored." (*The Unexpurgated Case against Woman Suffrage*, 1913).

A musical song of the times scoffed at the suffragettes:

> *Put me upon an island where the girls are few.*
> *Put me among the most ferocious lions in the zoo.*
> *You can put me on a treadmill, and I'll never, never fret.*
> *But for pity's sake, don't put me near a suffragette.*

The Kaiser's War

On August 4th, 1914, long-awaited war broke out with the Kaiser's Germany. Christabel Pankhurst wrote in *The Suffragette:* "As I write a dreadful war cloud seems about to burst. This then is the world as men have made it, life as men have ordered it . . . This great war is nature's vengeance . . . is God's vengeance upon the people who held women in subjection, and by doing that have destroyed the perfect human balance."

Once war had been declared both the W.S.P.U. and the National Union decided to concentrate their resources on helping Britain in its struggle with Germany. In 1914 Millicent Fawcett pledged in the suffragist paper *Common Cause*, that the National Union would support the war-effort:

"In the midst of this time of terrible anxiety and grief, it is some little comfort to think that our large organization, which has been completely built up during past years to promote women's

Above The First World War gave women many new social opportunities. For the first time there were bus conductresses.

Below Women working in engineering shops. They took the place of the men who had been called up

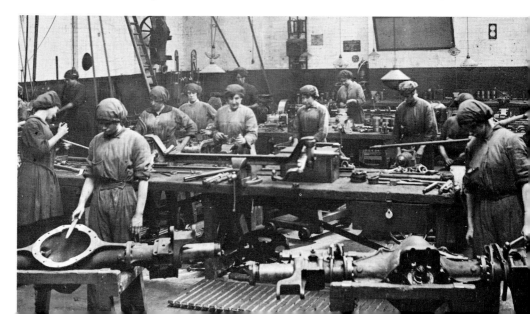

suffrage, can be used now to help our country through the period of strain and sorrow."

War work   The war opened up new opportunities for women to find work in factories, hospitals, and the public services. One trade journal noted that the work which women were doing was not "of the repetition type, demanding little or no manipulative ability." On the contrary, it was of the kind to tax "the intelligence of the operatives to a high degree. Yet the work turned out has reached a high pitch of excellence." *(Engineer,* 20th August, 1915).

Women became financially independent. As the *Daily Mail* reported: "The wartime business girl is to be seen any night dining out alone or with a friend in the moderate-priced restaurants in London. Formerly she would never have had her evening meal in town unless in the company of a man friend. But now with money and without men she is more and more beginning to dine out."

In consequence, their status began to change for the better; they grew more self-assured. The *New Statesman* commented in 1917 on the behaviour of the nation's war-time women workers: "They appear more alert, more critical of the conditions under which they work, more ready to make a stand against injustice than their pre-war selves or their prototypes. They have a keener appetite for experience and pleasure and a tendency quite new to their class to protest against wrongs even before they become 'intolerable'."

Nurse Edith   Women showed that they could equal men in deeds of bravery.
Cavell   In 1915 Herbert Henry Asquith, the Prime Minister, praised the heroism of Nurse Edith Cavell, executed by the enemy for helping Allied soldiers to escape from German-occupied Belgium: "She has taught the bravest man amongst us a supreme lesson of courage; and in this United Kingdom and throughout the Dominions of the Crown there are thousands of such women, but a year ago we did not know it." *(The Times,* 1915).

J. L. Garvin, a well-known journalist, confessed in the *Observer* in 1916: "Time was when I thought that men alone maintained the State. Now I know that men alone never could have maintained it, and that henceforth the modern State must be dependent on men and women alike for the progressive

OH! WHAT A SURPRISE!

Little Jack Horner sat in a corner,
    Eating Election pie.
He put in his thumb, and pulled out a plum,
    But *'twas not what he wanted*—oh my !

As this cartoon shows, politicians were still reluctant to give votes to
women, despite women's valuable services during the war years

strength and vitality of its whole organization."

Feminists believed that by their war-time activities women
were demonstrating that they were worthy of having the vote.
Mrs. Henry Morgan, a speaker at the Women Workers' Reconstruction Conference of 1915, said: "There is the much-
discussed question as to whether women are able to take part in
the defence of their country, and thus prove themselves worthy

111

to have a voice in its reconstruction. This oft-debated question has at last been settled by actions rather than words."

Millicent Fawcett   Next year Millicent Fawcett urged the Government: "When the Government deals with the franchise, an opportunity will present itself of dealing with it on wider lines than by the simple removal of what may be called the accidental disqualification of a large body of the best men in the country . . . We trust that you may include in your Bill clauses which would remove the disabilities under which women now labour.

"An agreed Bill on these lines would, we are confident, receive a very wide measure of support throughout the country. Our movement has received very great accessions of strength during recent months. Former opponents are now declaring themselves on our side, or at any rate withdrawing their opposition. The change of tone in the press is most marked . . . The view has been widely expressed in a great variety of organs of public opinion that the continued exclusion of women from representation will . . . be an impossibility after the war." *(Common Cause,* 19th May, 1916).

First women voters   The voting laws had to be changed to enfranchise soldiers who could not vote under the existing system. To the delight of suffragists and suffragettes alike, women were also accounted for in the new Bill. The Commons showed that it was in favour of women having the vote by a 7 to 1 majority, and the Lords, after three days of heated debate, by a majority of 63.

Jubilation   A jubilant Mrs. Fawcett wrote: "When I returned triumphant on the evening of 10th January (1918) from the signal victory of the Women's Suffrage cause in the House of Lords, feeling that women's (at least one woman's) place was home, within an hour interviewers began to arrive from various papers. One of them, knowing of my fifty years' association with the movement, asked me to describe briefly its 'ups and downs'. I said I could not do that, because it had been all 'ups' and no 'downs'. He looked so perplexed and incredulous that it is possible others may also regard my reply as misleading . . .

"The history of the women's movement for the last fifty years is the gradual removal of intolerable grievances. Sometimes the pace was fairly rapid; sometimes it was very slow; but it was

112

always constant, and always in one direction. I have sometimes compared it, in its slowness, to the movement of a glacier. But like a glacier it was ceaseless and irresistible. You could not see it move, but if you compared it with a stationary object and looked again after an interval of months or years, you had proof positive that it had moved. It always moved in the direction of the removal of the statutory and social disabilities of women. It established their individual liberty and freedom; they were in fact gradually passing from subjection to independence. That is why I said the history of the movement had been 'all ups and no downs'."

The Representation of the People Act (1918), though it enfranchised nine million women, restricted the vote to those who were aged thirty or over. The limit was imposed so that women would not become a majority of the electorate. Not until the Equal Franchise Act of 1928 were women placed in the same position as men regarding both parliamentary and local government elections. The total of women electors was then raised to 15,195,199, compared with 13,655,577 men.

As might be expected, these developments did not please everyone. In 1928 Lord Birkenhead, who was Lord Chancellor, told the House of Lords: "I'm against the extension of the franchise to women. I shall always be against the extension of the franchise to women . . . It was in the year 1918, after the War, that the disaster took place. Had it not been for the War, in my judgement we should have continued successfully to resist this measure for an indefinite period of time."

Lord Birkenhead

9 The Struggle Continues

AS WELL AS gaining the vote in 1918, women also became eligible to stand for Parliament. The first woman to take her seat in the House of Commons was Lady Astor (1879–1964). She later recorded: "Men whom I had known for years would not speak to me if they passed me in the corridors. They said I would not last six months. But I stuck it out." More than fifty years on, about 95 per cent of Members are still men.

Nancy Astor

In 1958 it was decided that the newly-established life-peerages would be conferred on both sexes. For the first time women entered the House of Lords. Lord Pethwick-Lawrence, who with his wife had been a staunch supporter of women's suffrage, wrote: "There they are in our midst, making speeches in the Chamber, joining in our committees and taking their part with us in all the intricacies and commonplaces of our daily life. All of them are women of wide knowledge and experience and everyone of them has made contributions of value and importance to our discussions. Needless to say they have not disturbed the decorum of the House or ruffled its susceptibilities. In a word, they have certainly made good."

But political emancipation did not bring the rewards that some women expected. Although British women enjoy more rights than those of their sex in many other parts of the world, they have not achieved complete equality with men. The law may still discriminate against them. A writer to *The Guardian* reported:

Women and hire-purchase

"Recently I went into a well-known furniture store, with the intention of ordering a bed to be paid for on hire-purchase terms. I was politely informed that I would have to bring my husband

115

Lady Astor the first woman to sit in the House of Commons, campaigning at Plymouth before the 1923 general election

"Battling" Bessie Braddock of Liverpool, for many years an active
Labour member of the House of Commons and supporter of the women's
rights movement

in 'to do the paper-work' as I would not be allowed to make the purchase myself without a guarantor, because I am a woman.

"I asked if the situation would be the same if I told them I was earning an independent salary. I was told that I would still need my husband to act as guarantor: I asked if my husband would need a guarantor; no, he would not. Poor Emily Davison. She died in vain." *(The Guardian,* 3rd February, 1967).

The *Robbins Report on Higher Education* (1963) showed that there were fewer women in universities than men and, with the exception of teacher-training colleges, they were in the minority in all spheres of higher education:

Robbins Report (1963)

"In the case of women, only 7·3 per cent of the age group entered all fulltime higher education in 1962, compared with 9·8 per cent in the case of men; if part-time education is included, the comparison is between just under 8 per cent for women and over 22 per cent for men. The difference is substantial . . . But the important point is that the difference between the sexes has its origin long before the age of entry to higher education. Although nearly as many girls as boys pass the General Certificate of Education at Ordinary level, many fewer stay on beyond this stage to take Advanced level . . . In 1962–63, a quarter of the students in British universities were women. In Training Colleges in England and Wales two thirds of the students were women."

There is still a widespread belief that women are uninterested in academic matters. Charles Curran, quoting Sir Robert Ensor, said: "Women in the mass have very little interest in doctrines, or arguments, or serious speculations of any kind. Their concern was not with ideas or principles, but with persons and things. Their main interest was in their feminine roles." *(The Spectator,* 19th November, 1965).

Women and politics

Sir John Newsom, who had recently been chairman of an important official committee on education, wrote in 1964: "The influence of women on events is exerted primarily in their role as wives and mothers, to say nothing of aunts and grandmothers. Even in employment outside the home, with the exception of schools and hospitals, this influence usually works by sustaining or inspiring the male. The most superficial knowledge of the way in which the affairs of Government, industry and commerce are

117

conducted makes this quite plain." (Sir John Newsom in *The Observer,* 11th October, 1964).

Although there are more than eight million women in employment in the United Kingdom, men retain control over most of the best jobs. In 1964 the National Council for Civil Liberties published a report, *Discrimination against Women,* which gave evidence of this:

"Law: 103 women practising barristers out of a total of 2,073 ... Just over 400 women were practising solicitors out of a total of 20,250.

"Accountants: 11,000 chartered accountants, 82 of them women.

"B.B.C.: When the survey was made, women held six of the 150 'top' jobs in the B.B.C. . . . .

"Journalism: About 2,000 women among the 18,000 members of the National Union of Journalists. There had never been a woman editor of a daily newspaper and even among the magazines which cater especially for women the majority of editors had been male.

"Medicine: 17 per cent of those on the Medical Register were women . . . Taking all medical students in all schools, just under 24 per cent were women and about 400 qualified each year . . .

"Dentists: 1,446 women out of 16,279 on the Register.

"Architects: About 700 women were working as architects, against 16,300 men.

"Civil Service: In the Civil Service as a whole there were 189 women in the Administrative class out of a total of 2,482; in the Foreign Service there were 23 out of 750. In the Executive class there were 358 women in the grades of Senior Executive Officer and above, out of a total of 4,326, and 598 out of 19,003 of equivalent level in the Professional, Scientific and Upper Technical classes . . .

"Finance and Commerce: Of 40,574 members of the Institute of Directors, only 850 were women."

The reason why so few girls took up scientific or technical careers, the *Economist* indicated, was not simply the result of "male ignorance and prejudice": "Anyone who wants to become a technologist or a scientist has to make his or her choice pretty early in life. Family attitudes, and the entire social ethos of a nation, and at least three generations of parents, teachers and pupils must be changed before it becomes regarded as normal for a young girl to aim at a career in industry." (29th August, 1964).

In many occupations a woman is paid less than a man, even though she carries out similar work: "It should be suggested to employers that, in the long run, paying women much less than men is a false economy; for if the pool of talent for responsible jobs is artificially small because the attraction of those jobs to women is minimised by low pay, this must mean that the increasingly inadequate pool of (almost exclusively male) labour trained for those jobs will be able to demand disproportionately high salaries." *Cry for equal pay*

Women's struggle for political equality has now given way to a struggle for economic equality. However, not all women support this cause. Lady Dartmouth, addressing a Round Table conference in 1965, spoke out strongly against mothers who work. The *Western Daily Press* reported her speech under the headline WORKING WIVES ARE SLAVES:

"Women doing a man's job without his physical stamina, rushing off in the morning, rushing home at night clutching the food which they must cook for supper, rushing to clean the house, rushing to cope with the children—there is only time for a quick kiss and a quick 'hello'. *"Working wives are slaves!"*

"Mothers today have no time to hear their children's problems or prayers.

"Wives have no time to tell their husbands, 'I love you'—but never mind, the instalments are almost paid on the new car."

Early in 1972 a Bill came before Parliament which was designed to end discrimination against women. *The Guardian* reported the debate on the Second Reading: *New bill (1972)*

"Noisy scenes occurred in the Commons yesterday during an unsuccessful attempt to get a second reading for the Anti-Discrimination Bill, which was 'talked out', and now stands little chance of further progress.

"The Bill's promoter, Mr. William Hamilton, had explained that the measure was modelled to some extent on race relations legislation. The Bill would set up an Anti-Discrimination Board.

119

"He accused Mr. Ronald Bell (Conservative, Buckinghamshire South) of describing women as inferior, second-class citizens 'who should be treated as such . . .'

"Mr. Hamilton said equal pay legislation would be completely ineffective unless women had equal opportunities in employment, training, education, and promotion. He said of the Women's Liberation Movement . . . 'having met some of them in the past week or two, I have been impressed by their intelligence, by their courage, by their determination, and by their courteousness . . .'

"Mrs. Joyce Butler (Labour, Wood Green) said the Bill arose because a bus conductress in a London garage saw a notice in the staff room encouraging staff to apply for training as an inspector. She applied and was told she could not be trained because she was a woman, and inspectors needed full experience of all aspects of the job including bus driving to qualify . . .

"Mr. Bell made sure that a vote could not be taken on the Bill by rising to speak a few seconds before 4 p.m., just as Mr. Hamilton rose to move the question be put on the second reading . . .

"Mr. Hamilton said emotionally: 'It is abundantly clear that 95 per cent of an unusually crowded House on a Friday is in favour of giving the Bill a second reading.'

"As the shouting at Mr. Bell continued, Mr. Hamilton, who was barely audible, said the women in this country would demand 'if not on this occasion, then very soon, that in the future this House will have the courage and guts to take a decision'." *(The Guardian,* 29th January, 1972).

Part of an article in *New Society* provides a fitting conclusion for this study. It asks: "Does society, as the feminist movement says, unfairly discriminate against women, or are women in some sense less qualified than men in areas of achievement? In a technological age, when physical prowess is less important, shouldn't women be expected gradually to assume equal status with men in all areas of achievement?"

The writers say that recent psychological research shows that there are real differences between the sexes. Only by acknowledging these can a satisfactory prescription be found for improving women's lot. The solution does not lie in "making women into men":

Opposite After winning electoral equality, women began to press for economic equality; members of the Civil Service Equal Pay campaign arrive to demonstrate at Caxton Hall, 1954.

"Rather it is necessary to change society to make its values less monolithic, and to change women to make them more free to pursue their interests and abilities in whatever direction they may lead.

"We should change the way we bring girls up, beginning in infancy, in order to encourage and make enjoyable achievement, independence and exploration; foster a realistic estimation of one's abilities and a sense of responsibility for one's actions; develop a wide range of interests which include 'masculine' as well as 'feminine' activities; provide opportunities for identification with fathers and brothers as well as with mothers and sisters; avoid defining a woman's value exclusively in terms of physical attractiveness or social skills.

"That society is best which enables the largest proportion of its members to contribute to it, and at the same time to attain self-fulfillment. It should be possible for a woman to have both a family and a career, to be a success as a wife and mother, as well as to achieve in a man's and woman's world." (Charles P. Smith & Carol H. Smith in *New Society,* 1st October, 1970).

Table of Events

1792 Mary Wollstonecraft: *A Vindication of the Rights of Woman.*

1832 Reform Act. Women excluded from the franchise.

1839 Custody of Infants Act.

1842 Coal Mines Act. Women and girls no longer allowed to work underground.

1847 Factory Act gives many women in factories a ten-hour working day.

1848 In United States, Seneca Falls Convention.

1850 Frances Buss founds North London Collegiate School for girls.

1857 Marriage and Divorce Act.

1859 Elizabeth Blackwell is first woman to be entered on British Medical Register.

1866 Cambridge local examinations opened to girls.

1867 Second Reform Act. John Stuart Mill fails to get it amended to give women the vote.

1869 J. S. Mill, *The Subjection of Women.*

1870 Mary Peachey denied a Hope Scholarship at Edinburgh University. First Private Member's Bill for women's suffrage, drafted by Richard Pankhurst.

1871 Women elected to London School Board.

1878 Women admitted to degrees of London University.

1884 Third Reform Act. Women still denied the vote.

1886 Deserted wife can sue husband for maintenance.

1888 Matchgirls strike.

1893 Women get the vote in New Zealand.

1897 National Union of Women's Suffrage Societies founded.

1902 Women get the vote in Australia.

1903 Women's Social and Political Union founded.

1905 First suffragettes imprisoned.

1906 Women in Finland get the vote.

1912 Emmeline Pankhurst imprisoned for conspiracy.

1913 Emily Davison killed on Derby Day.

1913 Women get the vote in Norway.

1918 Representation of the People Act gives vote to women of thirty and over.

1919 Nancy Astor is first woman to take her seat in the House of Commons. Women able to become barristers and solicitors, and to sit on juries.

1920 Oxford University admits women to degrees. Women get the vote in the United States.

1928 Equal Franchise Act.

1943 The large Amalgamated Engineering Union accepts women members.

1946 Royal Commission proposes equal pay for women civil servants, local government officers and teachers.

1948 Cambridge University admits women to full degrees.

1949 First woman King's Counsel.

1958 Creation of life peeresses.

1963 Robbins Report shows the number of women in higher education.

1966 First woman president of the British Association for the advancement of Science (Kathleen Lonsdale).

1972 Women's Anti-Discrimination Bill fails to get a Second Reading.

Further Reading

D. C. Brooks, *The Emancipation of Women* (Macmillan, London, 1970)

Eva Figes, *Patriarchal Attitudes* (Faber & Faber, London, 1970; Stein & Day, New York, 1970)

Roger Fulford, *Votes for Women* (Faber & Faber, London, 1958)

Kenneth Hudson, *Men and Women* (David & Charles, Newton Abbot, 1968; Transatlantic Arts, New York, 1969)

Josephine Kamm, *Rapiers and Battleaxes* (George Allen & Unwin, London, 1966; Humanities Press, New York, 1966)

F. Lamb and H. Pickthorn, *Locked-up Daughters* (Hodder & Stoughton, London, 1968)

Arthur Marwick, *The Deluge*, Chapter Three (The Bodley Head, London, 1965; Penguin, London, 1967; W. W. Norton, New York, 1970)

O. R. McGregor, *Divorce in England* (Heinemann, London, 1957)

W. L. O'Neill, *The Woman Movement* (George Allen & Unwin, London, 1969; Barnes & Noble, New York, 1969)

Christabel Pankhurst, *Unshackled* (Hutchinson, London, 1959)

E. Royston Pike, *Hard Times: Human Documents of the Industrial Revolution* (George Allen & Unwin, London, 1966; Praeger, New York, 1966)

E. Royston Pike, *Golden Times: Human Documents of the Victorian Age* (George Allen & Unwin, London, 1967; Praeger, New York, 1967)

E. Royston Pike, *Busy Times: Human Documents of the Age of the Forsytes* (George Allen & Unwin, London, 1969; Praeger, New York, 1970)

Marian Ramelson, *The Petticoat Rebellion* (Lawrence & Wishart, London, 1967)

Mary Richardson, *Laugh a Defiance* (Weidenfeld & Nicolson, London, 1953; Ambassador Books, Ontario, 1953)

Cecil W. Smith, *Florence Nightingale* (Constable, London, 1950; McGraw Hill, New York, 1951)

Ray Strachey, *The Cause* (Bell, London, 1928; Kennikat Press, New York, 1969)

Ray Strachey, *Millicent Garrett Fawcett* (John Murray, London, 1931)

Cynthia L. White, *Women's Magazines 1693–1968* (Michael Joseph, London, 1970; Humanities Press, New York, 1971)

Picture Credits

Index